UNAPOLOGETIC ATHLETE

CONFIDENCE, CLARITY & PURPOSE BEYOND THE GAME

Dr. Aren Joseph Ulmer

Unapologetic Athlete: Confidence,Clarity & Purpose Beyond the Game

Published by InnerGame Performance LLC Atlanta, Georgia, USA

ISBN: 979-8-9946649-1-9

Second Edition, 2026

The information in this book is based on the author's lived experiences and perspectives. Readers should consult qualified professionals for specific guidance.

10 9 8 7 6 5 4 3 2 1

Stay Connected:
Instagram: @dr.arenulmer
LinkedIn: Aren J. Ulmer
Unapologetic Athlete®

DEDICATION

To Whoever this makes sense for... Listen up. I know you think it's all about buckets and proving you're the best. But the game? It's just the training ground. One day, the crowd goes quiet, the jersey comes off, and you're left with the mirror. That's when you'll find out who you really are. Every cut, every benching, every night you felt slept on, that's not the end; that's the blueprint. You're built for more than stats. You're built for legacy. So, keep grinding, keep betting on yourself, and never apologize for the fire in you. Trust me!! You'll carry it further than the game ever could.

CONTENTS

INTRODUCTION

When I first realized I was more than an athlete, I didn't feel free. I felt lost.

All my life, the game had been my compass. It told me who I was, where I was going, and how I should show up every single day. From non-stop days in the Bay to my last game as an NCAA college athlete, my identity was stitched into a ball and a jersey. One that was so tightly wound that pulling on a single thread would unravel me entirely.

So, when it all stopped, the practices, the games, the noise, it felt like somebody had hit the mute button on my life.

Nobody prepares you for that.

Nobody tells you how to navigate the mental hurricane that comes with chasing greatness or what to do with yourself when the thing you've poured your soul into isn't there anymore.

That's why I wrote this book.

NOT A BLUEPRINT. A CONVERSATION.

This isn't one of those books that promises to fix your life in five steps or make you bulletproof with some magic mental formula. There are tons of those out there already.

I'm not here as the know-it-all expert either. I'm not here as a psychologist who's only studied this stuff in textbooks. I'm coming to you as a former athlete, a mentor, and most importantly, as a person who's still learning. A person who's still growing.

I've been through the grind, the wins, the injuries, and the self-doubt. I've seen the weight that comes with being "the one" everyone's counting on. And I've worked with athletes: high school, college, and professional; who've all wrestled with the same question in different ways:

Who am I beyond the game?

This book is my way of answering that question. Not with big, complicated words or theories, but with stories, tools, and reflections that actually make sense when life feels messy.

WHO THIS BOOK IS FOR

This is for the athlete grinding in an empty gym at 10 p.m., replaying every mistake in their head but still showing up tomorrow.

It's for the parent who wants to support their kid's dream without crushing their spirit.

It's for the coach trying to balance discipline and care in a generation that's wired differently.

And it's for the person who's no longer playing but still trying to figure out who they are without the game.

If you've ever felt like your worth was tied to your performance, this book is for you.

If you've ever wanted to master your mind, protect your peace, and live in alignment with your purpose, this book is for you.

WHAT YOU'LL FIND HERE

This book is split into four parts:

- **The Grind** – How the game shaped us, the lessons it taught, and the identity traps we fell into.

- **Where Hustle Meets Heart** – Tools for mastering your mindset, emotions, and inner game.

- **More Than the Game** – Navigating transitions, redefining success, and building a life that matters.

- **Soul Work** – A playbook for wholeness: faith, purpose, and unapologetic living.

Along the way, you'll hear not just my story, but the voices of others, athletes and mentors who've learned hard lessons and want to pass them on.

This isn't about revolutionizing the world or rewriting sport psychology. It's about helping. Helping you make sense of where you're at, giving you tools to move forward, and reminding you that you're not alone in the process.

UNAPOLOGETIC LIVING

The title says it all.

This isn't about being perfect. This isn't about being unbreakable. It's about showing up fully as yourself, mind, body, and spirit. It's about giving yourself permission to grow, to fail, to heal, and to win in ways that can't be measured on a scoreboard.

So, take what you need from these pages. Skip around if you want. Write in the margins. Sit with the questions. Share it with someone who might need it.

I'm not here to preach. I'm here to share.

This is your journey as much as it's mine.

Let's get started.

You ready?

PART I

THE GRIND

CHAPTER 1

THE COURT RAISED ME

The air in that Alameda gym was thick, like breathing through a wet towel. It was mid-summer, and the old building had no business trapping heat the way it did. The hardwood floor was slick with sweat, dust lingering in the air every time someone slid across it. Sneakers squeaked sharp against the floor, like nails on a chalkboard, the sound echoing through the space, mixing with the occasional swish of a made shot and the hollow clang of missed ones off a chipped backboard. Even the ball felt worn, smooth, almost slippery from the number of hands that had pushed it up and down the court.

We were thirteen, running on fumes after five or six games already, playing against a team of seventeen-year-olds who stepped onto the floor like they owned it. You could see it in their body language—shoulders high, voices loud, laughing like we weren't even worth their time. They weren't just here to win. They wanted to humiliate us. To make sure everyone in the gym knew we didn't belong on the same floor as them.

But for us, this wasn't about belonging. We didn't have the size. We didn't have the stamina. Hell, some of us could barely feel our legs anymore. But we weren't about to fold. Every cut, every screen, every loose ball; it was survival. That kind of survival where pride keeps you moving even when your body's screaming at you to stop. The older kids talked louder. We played harder.

And somehow, we stayed in it.

Every time they tried to break us, throwing elbows, bumping shoulders, or chirping after a bucket... we came right back. A steal here. A tough rebound there. It wasn't pretty, but it didn't have to be. One possession at a time, we clawed our way into their heads. By the fourth quarter, the laughs were gone. They were breathing heavy now, frustrated that the little kids weren't folding the way they expected them to.

When that final buzzer sounded and we were up by three, the gym fell silent for a moment. But as we walked off the floor, sweaty and worn down, something shifted.

We didn't just win a game.

We survived a test.

Looking back, I think that's where it started for me, the identity piece. This wasn't just basketball anymore. It wasn't just running plays and hitting shots. It felt bigger. Like suddenly there was a spotlight on us, and whether I realized it or not, it started to shape how I saw myself.

The game grew into something more meaningful. It now centered around proving something: to them, to the crowd, and maybe, most of all, to myself. That moment followed me off the court. And for years, I didn't even realize how much of my identity started to wrap itself around moments like that.

I still remember walking into the high school gym for my first summer workout as a freshman. I was 5'8", maybe 150 pounds soaking wet, staring at a group of upperclassmen who looked like grown men. Their shoulders were broader, their voices deeper, and the way they moved on the floor told you they weren't just hooping, they were playing with years of varsity experience behind them.

At fourteen, I wasn't supposed to be in the varsity conversation. Undersized freshmen rarely made that jump at my school unless they were special—the type of players who had college scouts sitting in the stands before they hit puberty. I wasn't that. But I wanted to prove I belonged.

That summer felt like war. Every drill was a test. Every scrimmage an opportunity for someone to humble me. I could feel the eyes on me, teammates sizing me up, coaches wondering if they'd wasted an invite, and even my own inner voice questioning whether I had any business being there. The physical stress was one thing. Running suicides with juniors and seniors who didn't even look tired. Getting knocked off balance by defenders twenty pounds heavier. Trying to finish through contact when my body hadn't caught up yet. Every night, I went home sore in places I didn't even know could get ache the way they did.

But the mental and emotional weight hit different. I was quiet in the locker room, afraid to say too much. I felt like an outsider trying to find his place. Some nights, I woke up replaying missed shots and turnovers, already dreading the next morning's practice.

Then, something changed. Subtly, but I noticed it, nonetheless. I stopped trying to play like I belonged and started working like I belonged. Hustle became my weapon. Diving for loose balls, sprinting back on defense, battling on the boards against bigger guys. Even if I got knocked down, I made sure they felt me. Little by little, respect came. Not because I was the most talented, but because I refused to quit.

By the time tryouts rolled around in the fall, I wasn't just fighting for a roster spot. I was fighting for minutes. And when the season opened and my name was called in the starting lineup, it didn't even feel real.

But with that moment came something I didn't expect. A shift in how I saw myself. Suddenly, I wasn't just Aren anymore. I was "the freshman starter." People in the hallways noticed. Teachers mentioned it. Even kids I'd never talked to gave me a nod and a quick dap.

It felt good, better than good, honestly. For the first time in my life, I felt like I was somebody.

But that feeling came with a cost.

When your identity becomes tied to performance, every game feels like a referendum on your worth. What should have just been labeled a bad night and nothing more instead felt like I was failing at being me. When I played well, the confidence carried over into everything. I was outgoing, loud, almost cocky. When I struggled, I retreated into myself. I felt small again. Invisible.

That identity started bleeding into my personality off the court. I wasn't just Aren the person, I was Aren the hooper. And while that opened doors and gave me purpose, it also left me with a question mark I couldn't shake:

Who was I without the game?

At the time, I didn't have an answer. So, I kept grinding. Kept trying to hold onto the identity I'd worked so hard to build. Because if I wasn't the kid who made varsity as a freshman, then who was I?

That question would stick with me for years.

Sophomore and Junior year came quick. Too quick.

That first season flew by like a blur—energy, noise, flashes of confidence and mistakes. And before I had time to settle in, the expectations were no longer the same. Coaches started looking at me differently. Not like a project or someone just happy to be there, but like someone they needed to count on. I wasn't the flashy recruit or the high scorer. I was the glue. The one they expected to do the little things, to hold things together when stuff got tight.

And for a while, I did.

I played my role. Hit open shots. Fought for boards. Hustled on every closeout. Took charges. You know, just trying to make the difference between a win and a loss. There were nights where I'd barely get noticed in the box score, but coaches would pull me aside after the game and say, "You made a difference tonight." That meant more to me than any stat ever could.

But what nobody talks about is how that kind of role comes with its own pressure. When you're the one who's supposed to "do the right thing" every time, there's no room for mistakes. I wasn't playing with house money anymore. I wasn't a freshman just trying to figure it out, I was expected to make the hustle plays, hit the open three, guard without being seen as a mismatch, and still stay out the way.

Some games, I felt locked in. Every rotation, every extra pass, every read came second nature. The game moved fast, but I felt even faster. But other nights, I'd be in my own head. One missed box out. One bad turnover. And I'd feel like the whole house was crumbling. When you're not the star, you don't always get the luxury of bouncing back with a heat-check. You just get benched.

I started to feel it before games—this pressure in my chest. Not the kind that fires you up, but the kind that makes it hard to breathe. Like I was tiptoeing through every possession, hoping not to mess up. Like I was auditioning every night just to stay in the rotation.

And the crazy part? From the outside, everything looked solid. Coaches trusted me. Teammates leaned on me. People said I was the "glue guy," the "heart of the team." But inside, I was running on empty. I was pouring into everyone else while quietly wondering whether I was enough. Whether I was playing my role up to standard. A role that had been prescribed for me. A role that I'd just accepted without pushback. A role that had fused with my very identity.

I remember walking through the hallway after a tough loss, one where I barely touched the ball but got cooked on a couple defensive possessions, and hearing someone say, "What does he even do out there?" They didn't mean it personal. But when you're the role guy, when your work often goes unnoticed unless it slips, it lands heavier.

So, I doubled down.

More reps. More film. More work. I wasn't chasing stats, I was chasing value. I needed to prove to myself that I mattered. That I was seen. That the effort added up to something.

But deep down, I was tired.

Not tired of the game, but tired of feeling invisible unless I was perfect. Tired of being the one who held things together, even when I was falling apart.

That's the thing nobody tells you when you build your identity around reliability, you stop feeling like you can ever afford to break.

And even when I started cracking... I kept showing up. Because that's what role players do. We carry the weight so others can fly. But I started to wonder: *What happens when the one who holds it all down needs someone to hold them?*

I didn't have an answer.

So again, I kept grinding.

By the time senior year rolled around, the balance had tilted.

I wasn't the wide-eyed freshman anymore, or the quiet sophomore trying to earn my minutes. I was the guy now. The captain. The voice in the huddle. The one diving for loose balls and then helping the younger guys up after. The one people looked at when things got tough. The one who didn't need to say much but said enough. And this team? This team had been through it with me. We weren't just hooping. We were hunting.

We weren't supposed to be in the conversation. Small school. No big-time names. No stars getting invited to elite camps or splashed on recruiting blogs. But we showed up. Played hard. Played smart. Played together. And then suddenly, we weren't just on the map. We were making noise. Noise that later turned into momentum. And momentum that later turned into something real. And just like that, we were on a Cinderella run to the state Final Four.

And for the first time in a long time, I wasn't playing to prove anything. I was just playing. Fully present. Fully alive. That love for the game, the reason I picked up a ball in the first place, came rushing back. I could feel it in warmups, in pregame talks, in the little moments during timeouts where the whole gym went quiet and it was just us, connected and locked in. It wasn't about pressure anymore. It was about passion.

Yeah, I still got in my head sometimes. Still replayed turnovers. Still wanted to be perfect. But it didn't control me like it used to. I could feel myself growing. Leading. Trusting. Loving the game again. Loving myself again, too. I wasn't scared to smile during games, to celebrate my teammates, to be emotional in the locker room. I knew who I was, and I knew I had earned that.

That senior season was healing in action. It was clarity. It was a reminder that you can fall out of love with something and still find your way back. And when you do? It carries a different weight.

Fast forward to college.

New level. New faces. New system. New expectations. And yeah, a little fear, too. Not the same kind of fear I had when I was trying to earn minutes as a freshman. This one was deeper. It was the fear of starting over. Of being unknown again. Of losing the rhythm I fought so hard to find. But I wasn't walking into this next chapter empty.

I was bringing all of it with me.

Every early morning workout. Every tough loss. Every huddle, every bruise, every silent moment of doubt. I was bringing the gym that raised me, the teammates that became brothers, the moments that nearly broke me, and the love that rebuilt me.

That court back home gave me more than just a jumper. It gave me perspective. It gave me roots. And now, I was ready to grow again.

It was a new season. A new chapter.

But the love? The love was the same.

CHAPTER 2

BASKETBALL, A SANCTUARY AND IDENTITY

The lights in the college gym burned bright like a stage, humming overhead as they reflected off the freshly waxed floors. You could see your own shadow moving beneath you on every cut, every jab step, like you were dancing with yourself. The scoreboard glowed red even when it wasn't on, and the rows of empty bleachers stood still like quiet witnesses to every rep, every breakdown, every whispered prayer. It was the kind of gym that felt sacred—not because of its history, but because of what it held. Pressure. Hope. Escape. Identity.

I had walked into that gym a hundred times, sometimes with teammates, sometimes solo. This time, it was just me. Backpack dragging behind me, hoodie half-zipped, headphones in but no music playing. The silence was louder than anything I could've queued up.

College life was already a grind. Early morning lifts before my body was even awake, classes that pretended my brain wasn't still fogged from practice, film sessions that broke down more than just my mistakes, but my confidence too. The group chats. The coach texts. The constant mental math of GPA, PT, who's watching, who's not. It all blurred together into one long performance.

But when I stepped on the court, even if just for a moment, the world slowed down. *My* world slowed down.

In here, nobody asked for your major. Nobody cared if you bombed your exam or fumbled a relationship. It was just you and the echo of the ball, bouncing through a space that made you feel like maybe, just maybe, you still had control.

The court had become my sanctuary long before college. But here, it felt like my lifeline. Therapy before I ever knew what therapy was. When the world asked me to be composed, articulate, and marketable, the game let me be raw. Angry. Free.

I'd run solo workouts in the off hours, telling myself I was outworking everyone. But truthfully, it was the only time I felt like I could breathe. The game gave me rhythm when life was offbeat. It gave me feedback when I didn't know how to ask for help. It gave me purpose when everything else felt like noise.

And early on, I fell in love with that transaction.

Work hard. Get better. Get seen.

But beneath that love was a truth I didn't want to face: I wasn't just playing basketball.

I *was* basketball.

I remember a night during my second year when the whole system started to crack. It was after a long week. Back-to-back games, multiple exams, a teammate going through something heavy that none of us had language for. The pressure wasn't just physical. It was in the air. In the locker room silences. In the way I had to wear my composure like armor because everyone else needed me to be "locked in."

I got a phone call walking out of the university campus center. I almost let it go to voicemail. But I didn't. And when I picked up, everything changed.

Somebody back home... someone I loved... was gone.

It wasn't expected. It wasn't fair. And the worst part was, I didn't have time to process it. Not really. There was practice that afternoon. Then film. Then recovery. Then a team meeting about travel for next week.

So, I did what I had trained myself to do. I shut it down. Put it in a box. Told myself, *Later.* Told myself the game would help me push through. That the gym would catch me when the world started spinning.

I walked into that same gym with the same lights, the same floors, but this time, it felt like all of it was too bright. Too exposed. I couldn't hide in it like I used to.

My shot was short. My legs felt heavy. My brain was trying to be in two places at once, and the court, my refuge, felt foreign.

I stayed anyway. Did every drill. Shot until my hands went numb. But the bounce of the ball no longer drowned out the pain. It only echoed it louder.

That night, sitting on the cold sideline, drenched in sweat I didn't earn, I realized something I never wanted to admit:

Even basketball couldn't save me this time.

Back when I was younger, it was different. I'd go to basketball camps and feel untouchable. Competing with kids from all over the country, locking in, putting on for the city. I remember one summer when I got pulled aside by a coach who said, "You've got that look—like you belong on a bigger stage." I held that moment close and fed off it. It became my much-needed fuel.

That validation, that sense of identity, turned into the foundation of how I moved.

If I wasn't smiling at home, I was focused.

If I wasn't talkative at school, I was locked in.

If I wasn't open emotionally, I was just carved out on my own terms.

But the truth was, I had started wrapping everything I was in this one thing. Basketball became the structure when it should've just provided it for me. The way I coped. The way I proved I mattered. That's what this game had turned into.

And it worked... until it didn't.

There was this one highly anticipated game. Two top programs in the state squaring off in front of thousands, alumni, and a major audience. The buildup had been loud all week since this was a rematch from a game in the previous season.

I tried to keep my routine the same. Pre-game music. Stretch. Lock in. Breathe. But my mind kept drifting back home. Back to that call. Back to who wasn't going to see this game. That void in my chest made it hard to stay grounded.

Still, I showed up. Hooped. Put up 14 points and 8 assists. Controlled the pace. Found open teammates. Did everything I was supposed to do.

And when the buzzer sounded, we walked away with the win.

But I didn't feel victorious. On the ride back home, tucked in a window seat, I stared out into the dark highway and thought:

Why do I still feel empty?

That game, more than any other, exposed the gap between performance and peace.

It proved that even on your best days, you can still feel lost.

That's when the unraveling began.

I stopped seeing the court as a sanctuary. Not because it changed, but because I had. Because the mask I wore to get through practice was now the same one I wore in everyday life. Because I started to realize that every time I said, "I'm good," I meant, "I'm surviving."

And surviving isn't the same as living.

I kept hooping. Kept grinding. But the deeper truth was beginning to take shape:

I didn't know who I was outside this game.

Nobody prepares you for the crash that comes when your identity is tied to performance. When your worth is linked to your last box score. And in college, that cycle is louder, faster, more unforgiving.

Your name becomes data.

Your presence becomes leverage.

Your image gets reposted, then critiqued, then forgotten if you don't keep producing.

And when the lights dim, and the cameras cut, and your phone is quiet, that's when the real questions hit:

Who am I if I don't start?

Who am I if I sit?

Who am I if I'm hurting and can't tell anybody?

Those aren't hypothetical questions. They're survival questions.

The depression didn't show up all at once. It crept in slowly. Missed meals. Early fatigue. Isolation that felt like a choice until it wasn't. Smiling through team dinners. Laughing at jokes I didn't hear.

And the worst part was, people thought I was doing great. Numbers were decent. Coaches said I had good energy. Trainers said I was locked in. But nobody asked how I was really feeling, and I didn't have the words to tell them even if they did.

Because when your whole life has been built around toughness, it's hard to admit when you're in pain.

And when your sanctuary stops feeling safe, you don't know where else to go.

But in that lowest season, when even the game couldn't hold me, I started to see what I'd been running from all along.

I wasn't just mourning a loss.

I was mourning a version of myself that had been built on survival.

I was grieving the kid who believed effort alone would heal everything. That if you just worked hard enough, focused long enough, you could outpace grief, loneliness, fear.

That version of me had served me well. But he wasn't built to last.

And slowly, I started letting go.

I began writing. Not for class. Not for coaches. Just for me. Scribbled notes. Random memories. Affirmation. Feelings I didn't know how to speak. I talked to a counselor on campus. Didn't tell anybody at first. Just went. Sat. Listened to myself say things out loud that I'd only ever felt in silence.

It wasn't magic.

But it was real.

And that mattered more.

I started reclaiming the game as my outlet. My craft. My canvas. A reflection of who I was, not the definition.

And in that shift, I found something new.

Not relief. Not instant peace.

But *honesty*.

And that became the foundation for my healing.

Now, when I walk into a gym, the lights still hum. The floor still shines. But I don't walk in needing the court to complete me.

I walk in whole.

I bring my grief. My growth. My laughter. My boundaries.

And the ball doesn't define me, it just moves with me.

It's a part of my story.

But it's not the whole book.

And for anyone reading this who's ever felt like the game was their only escape:

I see you.

You're not alone.

And you are more than this game—even when it doesn't feel like it.

Affirmation: *"Even when the court goes quiet, I still matter. Even without the jersey, I'm still here. Becoming more. Becoming free."*

CHAPTER 3

THE WEIGHT OF THE JERSEY

It starts with a name on the back, but the weight rarely lives there. It's on the front. The school, the city, the legacy. Every time an athlete pulls a jersey over their head, they carry more than their own dreams. They carry history. They carry pressure. They carry expectation.

There comes a moment when the game stops being just a game. When the sound of sneakers on the hardwood or the pop of a glove doesn't bring joy but responsibility. You're no longer just hooping for fun, you're performing. And you can feel that shift in your gut.

I've seen it in athletes across sports and levels. I've lived it myself. Doesn't matter if it's a nationally ranked hooper, a small college outfielder, or a former wide receiver now grinding in corporate sales. Once the jersey becomes a symbol of something bigger: family sacrifice, community pride, or someone else's lost dream, it starts to press into your skin. And you carry that weight everywhere.

And here's the thing: Pressure rarely announces itself loudly. It's not always in the coach yelling at you or the fans critiquing every play. Sometimes it's the long stare in the mirror before warmups, or that split-second of doubt before tip-off. It's knowing someone in the stands skipped work to be there. Or that your cousins are bragging about you back home even when you don't feel like yourself.

One client of mine was a high school point guard with heavy expectations. His community counted on him. They showed up to the games and watched him with anticipation and expectation. When his name was announced at home games, the gym erupted like he was already in the league. What they didn't see were the silent breakdowns. Sleepless nights. The way he started to dread practice because every missed shot felt like it let someone down. His anxiety didn't come from fear of the game, it came from fear of failing the people who had poured everything into him.

That's what the weight does. It chips away at the love. The same game that once gave you freedom now feels like a trap. And you can't say it out loud because what kind of athlete complains about success? What kind of man admits he's tired from carrying what everyone else considers a blessing?

You start to play tight. You avoid mistakes instead of chasing greatness. You rehearse your postgame interviews in your head before you even step on the field. And slowly, that pressure begins to numb the joy.

And this isn't just about sports. It's about identity. About growing up being the "one" in your family, your friend group, your neighborhood. About hearing phrases like "you're gonna make it out" before you even understood what that meant. As if your talent came with an expiration date—and if you didn't cash in, everybody else lost too.

There's one story I keep coming back to. A former football player I worked with. He didn't make it pro. Now he's selling tech and doing just fine. But every family reunion, someone brings up "how close he was." He told me, "Some days I feel like I'm not even allowed to move on. Like my whole life still revolves around something I didn't finish." He's wearing a suit to work, but deep down, he still feels like he's stuck in a jersey that won't come off, a second skin he can't shed, stitched too deep to peel away.

That's what makes this conversation so important. Because too many athletes are walking around smiling on the outside but suffocating underneath. They're told to be grateful, to be tough, to be quiet. But carrying other people's hopes with no outlet? That's a fast track to burnout, resentment, even depression.

So, what do we do?

We normalize saying it out loud: "This is heavy."

We create space where athletes can talk about the pressure without being labeled soft. We allow them to ask themselves: *Who am I playing for? Who am I trying to prove something to?* And if the answer isn't "myself," we help them find their way back. We help them realign their compass.

I often encourage athletes to reframe their relationship with the jersey. Not as proof they owe the world something, but as a reminder of how far they've come. Of who they've become. The jersey should never be a burden. It should be a badge. A signal of honor, not of debt.

It's okay to want to make your people proud. But not at the cost of your own peace. Not if it means losing yourself in the process.

Because at the end of the day, you were never just the jersey.

You've always been the one inside it.

And when it feels like the weight is too much to carry, pause and remember this:

You've earned the right to breathe. To be seen beyond the box score. To write your story on your terms. And that? No one can take that from you.

Affirmation: *I am not defined by the expectations placed on me. I am grounded in who I am becoming, not just what I represent. The jersey is a chapter, but I am the author.*

...

HEAVY IS THE CROWN – MEMOIR BY AARON MERCADEL III

The last time I picked up my football jersey, it felt heavier than ever. Each stitch carried a step on the journey to greatness. Each patch was like a stripe earned in battle for selfless deeds committed. The name stitched across the front wasn't just thread, it was a badge of honor, worn only by the toughest and most fearless. And when I put that jersey on, it felt like a talisman, unlocking a part of me capable of things far beyond comprehension. That jersey changed my life.

Before I ever stood in front of 18,000 fans on a field, I was performing for an audience...my family.

My father raised me to give 110% in everything I did. "I don't care if you're a janitor; you make sure you're the best and take pride in your work," he used to tell me when I was younger.

My mother, a praying woman, spoke scriptures over me my whole life. She made sure I had a relationship with God, so I'd have strength in my toughest battles.

My grandfather never let me get comfortable. "My grandson can beat your son in a race right now," he'd brag to other dads at the park.

And my great-grandmother, full of wisdom, taught me humility. "Just sit and watch for a while," she'd say. "You'll see, no one's better than anyone else. We're all just trying to figure it out."

At the time, it just felt like love. But really, my family was preparing me for sacrifice. Preparing me for a game that demands you give your all: compete every down, humble yourself, and have faith in something bigger than you.

The joy I felt knowing my family got to hear their last name repeated by announcers on game day? Unforgettable. Everything they sacrificed just so I could exist, that meant everything to me. I carried their love into every game.

But with that love came pressure. Not from them necessarily, but from myself. Every sprint, every play, every misstep either honored or disrespected what they had done for me.

Playing college football 1,700 miles from home gave me an even stronger sense of pride in where I came from: the block, the city, the people who watched me grow. I didn't just play the game. I had to represent. To show the world what Oakland, California, could do.

Coming home and hearing, "I knew you could do it" or "You show 'em how we get down over here" or "Just keep your head on straight" meant everything. So many people were counting on me to be the example.

I had to put on for my people who weren't as fortunate to even go to college or even live to see 18. I had to represent every inner-city kid with a ball and a dream. To them, I was the one who made it out. The one who changed the narrative.

That kind of belief can lift a man into space. But it can also weigh him down to the earth.

The chosen one has no room for failure. You mess up, and it feels like you've let the whole city down.

I was born into a culture where perseverance is mandatory. The Black community is full of stories where we start from the bottom. We don't cry about it, we find solutions. When things get hard, we go harder, because there's only reward on the other side.

And as my mother would say, repeating her favorite Black proverb: "What doesn't kill you can only make you stronger."

All these lessons showed up when I played. I was gritty. I worked hard. I pushed through any adversity without hesitation.

I was raised to never quit and to finish what I started.

That mindset, though fortifying, can also trap you in a cage. It makes you play through injuries, emotional stress, and mental fatigue. You keep going because looking soft isn't an option, even when you're breaking on the inside.

My culture gave me strength. But it also taught me to hide my pain. And that caught up to me more than once.

There were moments when I didn't love the game, not because I didn't love playing, but because I was drained by everything surrounding it.

Everyone expects greatness. Coaches. Fans. Family. Strangers. Even me. When you're up, everyone cheers. When you're down, they sit and watch. When you get injured, you risk being forgotten, or you fight through the pain.

Some games, I didn't play to win. I played just to avoid disappointing anyone.

It doesn't feel the same.

You start to wonder: Who am I without the jersey? Am I enough? Do they love me... or just what I can do?

In the beginning, the weight of my jersey defined me. Every win boosted my worth. Every loss chipped away at it. But over time, I realized the jersey wasn't made to break me. It was made to remind me.

A reminder of where I came from.

A reminder of what I've overcome.

A reminder of who poured into me.

That wisdom didn't make the weight disappear. But it gave it meaning.

I no longer had to carry the weight of the world alone.

I learned to play with love, not fear. With gratitude, not guilt.

I still wanted to win. I still wanted to dominate. But no longer to prove something. To honor something.

Sports is a revolving door. The cycle will continue. Somewhere, there's a 10-year-old kid sitting in the stands who will one day wear the jersey.

To them, I say this:

The weight is real. It's love disguised as pressure. Don't run from it, embrace it. It's about the name on the front more than the name on the back. But more important than both are the people who helped you on this journey. The ones who believed in you when you didn't believe in yourself. The ones who sacrificed time and money so you could chase something bigger than all of us.

Wear the jersey well. It doesn't have to be perfect. Just make sure you do it with heart.

The jersey is heavy.

But so is the crown.

CHAPTER 4

UNLEARNING "JUST TOUGH IT OUT"

In the Bay, showing emotion was considered weakness. As if being vulnerable was the same as handing someone the knife they'd later cut you with. We learned to take hits on the court and in life... and keep moving. To cover up any wounds, physical or emotional, because it was taboo to let anyone see you bleed. You didn't complain. You didn't cry. You didn't ask for help. That was the code. And if you did anything outside that code? You were soft. And in our world, soft didn't survive.

Growing up, toughness was currency. We wore it like armor. Whether it was physical pain, emotional weight, or mental stress, the answer was the same: keep pushing. Tape it up. Shake it off. Get back out there. Coaches praised it. Teammates expected it. Fans idolized it. Toughing it out became synonymous with leadership. With strength. With heart.

But the truth? That mindset is a double-edged sword.

Imagine you're in the middle of a high-stakes game. Your knee is screaming from a hit earlier in the quarter, but you stay in. You run through plays. You dive for loose balls. You ignore the pain, because you don't want the coach to sit you, or your teammates to question you. You convince yourself you're fine. Not because you are, but because you think you have to be.

Now shift the scene.

You just got some bad news from back home. Maybe someone passed. Maybe things at home are spiraling. But you're still showing up to practice. You're still locked in during games, doing everything you can to stay composed. And no one knows what's really going on. Because you've trained yourself to hide it all. Even from yourself.

That's what "tough it out" does. And most of us don't even realize it until the damage is already done.

We need to understand where this idea originates from. For so many of us, especially Black athletes, first-gen athletes, athletes from under-resourced communities, toughness is survival. When your life off the court is chaotic, showing weakness feels like a luxury you can't afford. You learn to compartmentalize early. You learn to suppress. Because there's no safety net. No room to be anything less than resilient. You carry expectations, dreams, burdens—sometimes for yourself, sometimes for your whole family.

And the sports world doesn't challenge that. It feeds it.

Watch any pregame montage. Watch how we glorify the athlete who plays through a torn ligament, who comes back too early from a concussion, who silently battles depression but "still shows up." We don't just admire that; we reward it. You get more playing time. More respect. You get labeled a warrior. And let's be real: there's pride in that. There's pride in being dependable, in being the one who never folds.

But over time, that pride can turn into a prison.

And what happens when you make toughness your only gear? Whether it's a torn hamstring or a shattered sense of self-worth, pushing through without tending to the injury only makes things worse. You might think you're hiding it, but your game shows it. Your body shows it. Your energy shows it. The constant pressure to "be okay" is exhausting. Always having to keep your guard up, always performing, never pausing to process, and that simply wears you down. And the moment you finally hit a wall, it feels like everything crashes at once.

And it's not just about performance. When you're always in tough-it-out mode, you become emotionally unavailable. Teammates, friends, family, they can't reach you. You're there, but you're not. You isolate yourself to protect the image, but deep down, you're lonely. When being tough becomes your entire identity, what happens when you can't be tough anymore? Who are you when you're injured? When the season ends? When you finally admit you need help?

I know this all too well. There was a time when I was hurting, and I still showed up like nothing was wrong. I laughed. I trained. I competed. And then one night, everything caught up. I sat in my room, lights off, just numb. No game to focus on. No crowd to distract me. Just me and the truth I kept outrunning. That night taught me something: toughness without vulnerability isn't sustainable.

I used to think toughness meant staying silent and pushing through. But that wasn't strength. That was fear dressed up as pride. And the more I lived that way, the more disconnected I felt from the parts of me that needed healing. The culture surrounding me didn't teach me that toughness could coexist with softness. I had to learn that on my own, all while unlearning what I thought I knew. What I thought was truth.

Toughness isn't the absence of emotion. It's the ability to feel and keep going. It's not silence. It's knowing when to speak up. It's not pretending you're fine. It's having the courage to say, "I need a minute." That's real strength.

Some of the most elite athletes in the world are now openly talking about therapy, mental health breaks, and boundaries. That's not weakness. That's leadership.

That's evolution. And as the next generation, we owe it to ourselves to shift the culture forward.

Unlearning takes work. It takes intention. It takes denouncing generations of survival mechanisms passed down like playbooks. But it's worth it. Because once you stop pretending, you start healing. You start reclaiming parts of yourself that have been quiet for too long.

So, how do we even begin that process?

First, awareness. Pay attention to the moments you're "toughing it out." What are you really feeling? What are you afraid will happen if you speak up or slow down? That self-honesty is the first crack in the armor.

Then look at who you keep around you. Who reinforces the idea that you have to be unbreakable? And who gives you permission to be real? You need people who see you, for you! Not just your stats, or your image.

Find a space to talk. That might be therapy. It might be a mentor or a coach who gets it. But you need somewhere you can be unfiltered. Somewhere you don't have to perform. Somewhere you can say the things you usually bury.

Start rewriting your internal script. Instead of saying "I'm good" when you're not, try, "I'm managing" or "I'm figuring it out." Give yourself room to feel without shame. It's a small shift, but it makes a big difference.

Create space in your routine for check-ins. It could be journaling before bed, five minutes of stillness after practice, or even voice notes to yourself. Ask: How am I really doing? What's weighing on me? What do I need right now? That regular reflection helps you build a relationship with yourself beyond performance.

And if you're in a position of leadership, whether it is on your team, in your friend group, wherever, be the one who goes first. Normalize talking about mental health. Model vulnerability. Make it cool to care about your wellbeing.

The game has evolved. Now it's our turn to evolve with it.

I used to think resilience was about never breaking. Now I know it's about learning how to bend and not snap. About pausing when you need to, so you can come back stronger. About knowing the difference between pain that builds you and pain that breaks you.

So, let go of the "just tough it out" badge. You don't need it anymore.

You got something better now.

Real resilience. Real clarity. Real freedom.

You.

If you're reading this and you're young, gifted, and grinding, hear me. You don't have to prove your worth by how much you can endure in silence. You don't have to sacrifice your mental health just to stay on the floor. You are allowed to feel. You are allowed to rest. You are allowed to ask for help. That doesn't make you soft. It makes you smart. It makes you sustainable. It makes you a better athlete, a better teammate, a better person.

...

MARCH MADNESS – MEMOIR BY KYREE BROWN

March 2023 was supposed to be the pinnacle of my college basketball career. Instead, it became the month that showed me the difference between playing a game and living a life.

We had just beaten Bryant University in the quarterfinals on March 4. The arena was packed, the crowd electric, my teammates soaring, and I felt invincible walking off that court. The semifinals were set for March 7, with March Madness waiting just beyond. That night, I fell asleep like a champion, dreaming of banners, legacies, and moments that would live forever.

The next morning began like any other: breakfast, film session, treatment at the facility. Everything felt normal. My teammates were grinning, the energy contagious. We were one step closer to everything we had worked for. After treatment, I grabbed my phone to find five missed calls from a childhood friend. My stomach sank before I even called back. His voice broke through tears: "Ju's gone, man. He's gone."

The words hit me like a freight train. My brother, not by blood, but by every bond that mattered, was gone. Just hours earlier, I had been on top of the world, and now, the floor had vanished beneath me.

The day before, Ju had texted me after catching the end of our game. "So proud of you, bro. Keep doing your thing." He told me how much purpose he found working with kids at the Hayward Rec, how their smiles lit up his world. That was Ju. Always making others laugh, always spreading joy. The cruelest irony was that he gave so much light to others, yet somehow, his own darkness overtook him.

None of it made sense. We were supposed to celebrate together. I was supposed to call him in a few days to tell him we were heading to the championship. Instead, I was sobbing in a training facility, begging God for answers that never came.

The walk from the locker room to the gym that day was the longest of my life. My teammates buzzed with championship energy while I fought to keep my grief from spilling over. When my coach asked if I could practice, his words cut even deeper. "Your friend died?"

Friend?

No. My brother. The kid who had been there since first grade, who knew me better than anyone. I wanted to scream every curse I knew, but the weight of my sadness kept me silent.

I locked myself in the bathroom, yelling at the mirror until a stranger's broken face stared back. Somehow, I pieced myself together enough to function, but inside, I was shattered.

By March 7, the semifinal game had arrived. I hadn't slept. All day I played his music on repeat. "9 Letters." Just to hear his voice one more time. When the ball tipped, I poured everything into those forty minutes: the anger, the heartbreak, the confusion. I gave it all I had, but it wasn't enough. We lost. My teammates wept as their dreams slipped away, but I had no tears left.

For years, basketball had been life or death to me. But after losing Ju, the game's meaning shifted. Compared to real death, a loss on the court felt small. Strangely, that realization gave basketball back to me. It became my sanctuary again, not because winning was everything, but because playing meant I was still alive, still fighting, still honoring the brother who believed in me until his last day.

Ju would have wanted it that way. He always helped people find joy, and I knew he would want me to find mine.

This was the real March Madness for me, a month that changed me forever. Some games change a season. Some change a career. But those days in March changed my soul, teaching me that the truest victories aren't measured in points or banners, but in how we carry forward the love of those we've lost.

WHERE HUSTLE MEETS HEART

CHAPTER 5

SMART > TOUGH

All my life, I believed the grind was enough. That if I just pushed harder, worked longer, or locked in more than the next guy, I'd be good. In sports, that mindset gets rewarded early. Hustle culture loves effort. Coaches praise toughness, fans love a comeback story, and teammates lean on you when they know you won't fold. But what do you do when hard work isn't the answer?

When I missed the game-winner, wide open, top of the key, I didn't lack effort. I wasn't unprepared. I had put in the reps. I had done the visualization. I had iced my legs and dialed in all week. But the shot rimmed out. And in the locker room after, with the towel over my head, it hit me: toughness had no answer for that moment.

This isn't about being soft. It's about being smart. Because the strongest athletes I've worked with? They're not the ones who just gut it out. They're the ones who adapt. The ones who know when to pivot, how to regulate their emotions in real time, and when to let go of control and lean into the chaos. That's power.

Growing up, you learn to survive through force. Like I mentioned earlier, showing emotion was weakness. Admitting something bothered you was out of the question. You lace 'em up and handle your business. Period. Sure, that mindset might build resilience, but it also builds silence. And silence, over time, leaves you stagnant. The more we train ourselves to "tough it out," the less we learn to adjust. And that becomes dangerous when life throws curveballs that strength alone can't catch.

This is where the idea of psychological flexibility comes in.

Psychological flexibility is the ability to stay present, make room for uncomfortable emotions, and still move toward what matters. It's not about avoiding pressure. It's about choosing how you respond to it. Let me say that again: Choosing. How. You. Respond.

In athlete terms, you know how your body has to adjust to different defenders, different speeds, different conditions? Your mind has to do the same thing.

Flexibility over force. Always.

I work with a lot of athletes who have been conditioned to be reactive. A bad play? They snap. A coach benches them? They spiral. A teammate misses a switch? They throw their hands up. But flexibility is about interrupting that loop and checking in with yourself: *What's actually needed from me right now?*

Sometimes it means calming down. Sometimes it means speaking up. Other times, it means letting the emotion move through you without attaching to it. That's mindfulness. That's acceptance. That's adaptation in real time. And this extends off the court, too. It leaks into everyday life, where we need to learn to pause before speaking, to listen before defending, and to understand before reacting.

One thing I always have to re-teach: emotional control isn't the same as emotional suppression. Being smart mentally doesn't mean you stop feeling things. It means you stop fighting them. Pain? It's part of the process. Doubt? That's normal. Anger? It's information.

When athletes learn to create space between stimulus and response, they unlock a new level of composure. Not because they're emotionless, but because they're no longer controlled by emotion.

One athlete I worked with a high-profile quarterback, and he used to throw a tantrum every time he missed a throw in practice. Not because he was immature, but because he thought anger was a performance tool. It took weeks, but once we unpacked that notion and gave him space to observe his reactions without judgment, everything shifted. He didn't stop caring. He just stopped crumbling under pressure. And the results followed.

I'm not anti-grind. Don't get it twisted. There's honor in showing up, in consistency, in giving more than what's asked. But the grind alone is incomplete. The real edge comes when you combine effort with awareness. Think about it like this: hard work gets you to the game. Adaptability keeps you in it.

Life doesn't always follow your game plan. That transfer you didn't see coming. That injury in the middle of your peak season. That breakup right before playoffs. That unexpected benching. Flexibility gives you room to adjust, to shift, to respond. It becomes your bounce-back muscle. And that muscle needs training.

I never hand athletes a worksheet labeled "Psychological Flexibility." But here's how I sneak it in. I teach breathwork not as a luxury but as a weapon. A few rounds of box breathing between plays? That's recovery in real time. It centers you. It slows your reactive brain. It gives you back control.

When athletes are struggling with motivation, I don't throw consequences at them. I ask, "What type of teammate do you want to be today?" or "What would your future self thank you for?" That small shift from punishment to purpose? That's a commitment to values.

Whether it's nerves, frustration, or fatigue, I invite athletes to say it out loud. "I'm anxious." "I'm annoyed." "I'm not focused." Naming removes the shame. It clears space. And from that space, we choose the next action.

We run mental walkthroughs just like film sessions. But instead of just Xs and Os, we review internal plays: What came up for you in that moment? What did you do with that thought? What could you try next time? This builds a relationship with your inner world.

But let's get something straight. Adapting doesn't mean abandoning. Flexibility isn't an excuse to quit or avoid discomfort. In fact, it demands you lean into the challenging stuff, just with better tools. Adaptation is strength. It's adjusting the sails when the wind shifts.

I had an athlete come to me after getting benched halfway through the season. He was angry, embarrassed, and ready to transfer. But after a few sessions, we reframed it: What if this was a test of growth, not talent? What if the bench was a mirror, not a punishment? He stayed. He adjusted his role. He became the energy guy. The guy who knew every teammate's tendency. The guy coaches trusted late in games because he never pouted. By postseason, he was back in the lineup, and better than ever. He didn't get tougher. He got smarter.

Think about an area of your life right now where force isn't working. Where pushing harder has only left you stuck or exhausted. What would it look like to shift from grinding to guiding? To respond instead of react? Take a breath. Write it down. You're not quitting. You're adapting.

Here's the thing nobody tells you: The world outside the game doesn't reward the toughest. It rewards the most flexible. Jobs shift. Relationships change. Your body ages. Goals evolve. The people who thrive aren't the ones who resist those shifts. They're the ones who move with them, while staying grounded in who they are.

That's what psychological flexibility really is: awareness of your inner experience, acceptance of the uncomfortable, and action toward your values. Even when it's hard. Especially when it's hard.

Remember, smart is greater than tough. Not because effort doesn't matter, but because effort without direction is wasted energy.

I think back to one of my favorite athletes I've worked with. A pro hooper overseas. He was a bucket, no question, but early in his career, he burned out fast. Every mistake felt like the end of the world. Every setback was an identity crisis. We worked together for months on the basics: mindfulness, values, self-compassion. He started journaling. Started meditating. Started watching film not just to critique plays, but to study his patterns.

And one day, after hitting a career high, he didn't celebrate like he used to. No chest pound. No screaming. Just a smile, a nod, and a walk back to the locker room. I asked him about it later.

He said, "I'm not chasing validation anymore. I'm just showing up for the moment."

That's it. Not harder. Smarter. Not tougher. Truer. Let go of the myth that pushing through is the only way. Learn to pause, pivot, and press on with intention.

That's real strength. That's the athlete who lasts.

Affirmation: "I bend, I don't break. I adapt, I don't avoid. I choose growth, even in chaos."

CHAPTER 6

BRICK X BRICK CONFIDENCE

All throughout my early playing days, I thought confidence came externally. Praise from a coach. Likes on an Instagram clip. A hot streak during the season. When I played well, I felt good. When I didn't? Everything crumbled. I was addicted to approval, a quiet obsession that looked like ambition on the surface, but underneath was really just insecurity in disguise. There was no intrinsic motivation lacing my actions. There was no internal dialogue keeping me going. I relied on factors outside myself, factors I couldn't control. Factors that would eventually let me down and wear me out.

Nobody tells you how easy it is to confuse applause with confidence. But they're not the same. One fades when the noise stops. The other stays rooted, even in silence.

The first time I really felt that difference was after a big game where I dropped double digits in the second half. People were excited, coaches were nodding my way, and I remember thinking, *Okay, I'm finally here.* But the next game? I was off. And it didn't just feel like a bad day, it felt like I had lost all the ground I thought I gained. That's when it clicked. I wasn't actually confident. I was just on a high.

Confidence built on outcomes is shaky by nature. It rises and falls with every stat sheet. But confidence built on intention, process, and self-trust? That's different. That sticks.

Real confidence is boring. It looks like reps. Like early mornings. Like studying tendencies. Like not needing a camera or a caption. It's brick by brick. Not flashy. Not fast. But permanent.

You know who gets this better than most? Musicians. Especially artists who have had to grind without a label, without radio, without a cosign. Think about someone like Russ. Love him or hate him, his come up is a blueprint for internal confidence. He released songs every week for years with little to no traction. No major features. No big budget. Just belief. And that belief was built through consistent output. He trusted the process long before the industry started clapping.

Confidence grows when you do the work without needing the world to notice.

The music industry's full of people who look confident because they're draped in success. But take away the followers, the streaming numbers, the headlines, and you see who really knows themselves. Same thing with athletes. Or actors. Or entrepreneurs. When everything is stripped down, can you still stand in who you are?

I ask my athletes this all the time: *Who are you when you're not performing?*

If the only time you feel valuable is after a win, we've got some work to do.

So, let's break it down. Performative confidence is built on reactions. Real confidence is built on values. Performative confidence needs validation. Real confidence creates it from the inside out. Performative confidence is loud. Real confidence doesn't need to say much at all.

One of the ways I teach this is through something I call "confidence stacking." It's the idea that every time you keep a promise to yourself, you add a brick. You said you'd get up early to stretch? Brick. You journaled even when you were tired? Brick. You stayed focused during practice even though your role was limited? Brick.

Confidence is built in those small moments. The ones nobody claps for. And over time, those bricks create a foundation that no one can shake. Because it's not about what they say. It's about what you know.

There's also a myth I like to break with athletes: the idea that confidence means never doubting yourself. That's not true. Even the greats question things sometimes. The difference is, they don't *stay* there. They have tools to bounce back.

One of my favorite reframes goes like this: "You don't need to feel confident to act confident."

Confidence isn't always a feeling. Sometimes it's a decision.

When I work with athletes who are in a slump, we zoom in on behavior, not emotion. What does a confident version of you do in this situation? How do they walk, talk, breathe, show up? Then we act from that space, even if it feels awkward at first. Confidence catches up to consistency.

Another practice I use is what I call "mirror moments." Not the motivational ones where you shout affirmations. These are quieter. Honest. Intentional. At the end of the day, I ask athletes to look in the mirror and ask: Did I show up today with integrity? Did I stay connected to my values? Did I put in the work I said I would?

If the answer is yes, that's your confidence cue. If the answer is no, cool. Adjust tomorrow. No shame. Just realignment.

Confidence also grows when you stop tying your worth to performance. You are not your stats. You are not your minutes. You are not your last game.

You are you. Period.

One of my athletes, a young hooper out of the Midwest, used to lose it every time he had an off night. Not just in frustration but in identity. He felt like a failure because the box score didn't match his standard. We worked on how to separate the player from the person. Who he is versus what he does. Now, even when he has a rough game, he says, "That wasn't me at my best, but it doesn't touch who I am."

That kind of self-talk? That's real confidence.

We don't build it by pretending we never struggle. We build it by learning how to talk to ourselves when we do. Because why hide it if we all struggle? Why pretend it isn't happening when facing it head-on is what actually makes us strong.

I think back to when I went to a Kendrick Lamar concert. The room was electric, thousands of voices in sync, but it still felt like each person was having their own private conversation with the music. That's the thing about Kendrick, he doesn't just perform, he holds up a mirror. Later, while running back some of his throwbacks, that same feeling came over me. And it reminded me of the kind of confidence it takes to build something brick by brick.

When Kendrick dropped *Mr. Morale & The Big Steppers*, it wasn't designed for quick approval. It wasn't the type of album you throw on for background noise or to catch a hit single. It was raw, heavy, layered, uncomfortable at times. He laid out his flaws, his pain, his accountability. It wasn't easy to digest, but it was honest. That's what stood out. He wasn't chasing streams or trying to manufacture a chart-topper. He was chasing truth.

That's what it looks like to trust the foundation you're building. Not rushing for applause, not cutting corners for validation, but stacking each brick with intention, even if people don't understand it right away. If you haven't listened to that album front to back, I encourage you to do it. Not casually. Sit with it. Let it hit you the way real art should. You'll feel what it means to stand firm in your message. That's the same kind of confidence it takes to build your life, your career, your identity brick by brick.

So, when I talk to athletes about building confidence, I remind them: it's not just about hype videos and game winners. It's about who you become when the camera is off. When the gym is empty. When nobody is watching.

Brick by brick.

Wake up early when it's easier to sleep in? Brick. Hold yourself accountable without needing someone to check on you? Brick. Keep your routine on tough days? Brick.

You don't borrow confidence. You build it.

And here's the beautiful part: the more you build it, the less you need the world to validate it. Because you've got receipts. You've got evidence. You've got that quiet, grounded sense of knowing who you are, regardless of what the scoreboard says.

So, here's your reflection: What's one small promise you can make to yourself today? And how will you keep it?

Start there. Then do it again tomorrow. And the next day.

That's how confidence is made. That's how it lasts. That's how you stop performing and start becoming.

You already have what it takes. Now go lay that next brick.

CHAPTER 7

STILLNESS IN THE STORM

The gym was packed. Fourth quarter. Playoff game. Tension high enough to rattle bones. Picture yourself courtside. The buzz in the arena is deafening as students chant, coaches' pace, and parents grip the edge of their seats. The score is tight. One possession could change everything.

Now lock in on a player, a young guard, number 11. You've seen him dominate all season, but tonight, he looks... different. The ball swings to him at the top of the key. You can see the hesitation just before the shot. Not in his body, but in his breath. It's shallow. Rushed. He pulls up. Shoots. And it's not close. A hard brick off the back rim.

He jogs back on defense, but his body language has shifted. His shoulders tighten. Jaw clenched. Eyes darting, not focused. You can almost feel what's going on inside his head. That single moment starts to spiral. He gets beat on the next possession. Starts barking at a teammate. His whole presence is different.

Now go back and really visualize what you just read. Write yourself into this script.

It wasn't a lack of skill. It was a lack of stillness.

So many athletes think pressure is about rising to the occasion, but it's really about *settling into it.* Owning the moment without letting it own you. And that only happens when you train your inner game as hard as your outer one.

Stillness in the storm. That's what makes all the difference.

When things get chaotic: bad calls, crowd noise, missed shots, trash talk, momentum swings—your nervous system gets hijacked. It happens fast. Your breath shortens. Your shoulders tighten. Your awareness narrows. And without a reset button, you're not making decisions anymore. You're reacting. Operating from survival mode, not performance mode.

The athletes who last? The ones who rise in high-pressure situations? They don't just have strong bodies. They have calm minds.

I once worked with a pro tennis player who was notorious for getting in her own head during tiebreakers. Her serve would go from fluid to stiff. Her body language would shift, and her opponents could see it. She knew what to do physically, but mentally, she was drowning.

We didn't overhaul her technique. We taught her how to reset. One breath. Two feet on the ground. One deep exhale. One phrase she repeated: "Here now."

She wrote it on her wristband. Every time her mind drifted, she used it to come back. It didn't make her invincible. But it made her present. And that presence started winning points she used to give away.

That's the thing about stillness. It's active. It's a skill. You can't push it off to the side, even if you try.

I talk to athletes all the time about learning to stay in their bubble. Your bubble is your space of control. Everything inside it: your breath, your thoughts, your reactions, your focus—that's yours. Everything outside? Crowd noise, opponent antics, ref decisions, expectations? That's not yours.

Staying in your bubble means protecting your mental real estate.

There's something powerful about the athlete who doesn't flinch.

We see it in different sports, different moments. Think about Shelly-Ann Fraser-Pryce on the track. Her starts are explosive, but her face? Always composed. Her ability to stay locked in before the gun goes off is a masterclass in mental presence. That calm right before the burst? That's stillness. Or Naomi Osaka, who brought her breathwork routines to center court and showed the world what composure could look like in real time. Or even surfers like Carissa Moore, waiting for the perfect wave, completely in tune with the ocean, reading patterns that most of us miss because we're too busy trying to control everything.

These athletes aren't calm because they don't care. They're calm because they've trained for chaos.

So, how do you train for chaos?

First, you stop avoiding discomfort.

The breath you take when your heart is pounding? That's a rep. The pause you take before reacting to a bad call? That's a rep. The choice to stay locked in when your team is down double digits? Rep.

Second, you build internal reset routines, repeatable habits grounded in science.

Research shows that deep, rhythmic breathing helps regulate your nervous system, calming the stress response and bringing your brain back online. I teach athletes quick reset routines that might include:

- Three grounding breaths using box breathing.
- A physical anchor, such as tapping their leg or pressing their feet into the floor.
- A short mental phrase like "I'm locked in" or "Next play."

These routines are subtle. But when practiced consistently, they become powerful. They remind your body and brain: that you're in control.

And when mistakes happen, because they will, we don't freeze. We reset. Here's a tool I give athletes: the five-second window. You give yourself five seconds to acknowledge the mistake. You name the emotion if it helps: frustrated, distracted, tight. Then you shift. Breathe. Focus. Move. Back to the task.

Stillness means *you* move with intention.

And here's why that matters. When your nervous system gets hijacked, your prefrontal cortex, the part of your brain responsible for decision-making—starts to shut down. Your body goes into fight, flight, or freeze. That's biology and shouldn't be mistaken for weakness. But here's the good news: you can train it.

Through breathwork, mindfulness reps, and emotional regulation practice, you build up what scientists call interoceptive awareness, or in normal terms, your ability to recognize internal signals and use them. It's not just about taking a breath. It's about understanding what that breath is doing: lowering cortisol, bringing clarity, and giving you back choice.

Athletes often ask me, "What if I lose my edge if I get too calm?"

I remind them: intensity isn't the enemy. Unregulated intensity is.

There's nothing wrong with emotion. But emotion needs a container. Stillness is just that. It holds your fire without letting it burn you.

So, here's the real question: *When the game gets messy, who are you?*

Can you find your breath when the noise gets loud? Can you come back to the moment when everything around you is trying to pull you out of it? Can you lead with calm, even when you're not sure how things will play out?

Because that's the edge. That's the separator. That's the type of presence that shifts momentum.

And you don't need to be a pro to access it. You just need to train it.

Start small. Right now, take a deep breath. Feel your feet on the floor. Exhale slowly. Say to yourself, "I'm here. I'm okay. I'm ready."

Do that daily. Before practice. Before class. Before hard conversations.

Make stillness your superpower.

Because the storm will come. It always does.

But the calmest one in the room? That's usually the one who leads.

Think of your mind like water. Calm water reflects clearly. Stirred-up water distorts everything.

The goal isn't to never feel the ripple. It's to know how to return to center.

That's stillness in the storm. That's the real game.

Before we close out this chapter, you'll hear directly from doctoral candidate Demond Washington in the next section. His journey with emotional regulation is one of the most powerful examples I've seen. He didn't start out with some monk-level mindset or perfect poise. He was fiery, raw, and reactive, and sometimes it cost him. But instead of hiding from that struggle, he leaned into it. He learned the tools, embraced the setbacks, and started mastering his response in pressure moments. Not overnight. Not all at once. But brick by brick. His story isn't just inspiring, it's proof that stillness can be trained.

...

SAME PLAYER, DIFFERENT JERSEY – MEMOIR BY DEMOND WASHINGTON

Where do I begin? This is the first time I've truly sat down to reflect on two of the most important identities in my life: the former athlete and the current therapist. I call this chapter "Same Player, Different Jersey."

As the saying goes, experience is the best teacher. That truth holds up in every corner of life, and especially in mine. But what no one tells you is how hindsight becomes the lens that sharpens those lessons. It's almost unfair that the clarity comes later, after you've already lived through the struggle. The cycle repeats itself with every person, every athlete, every story.

Basketball taught me more than just how to run plays or hit shots. It gave me micro-skills, life skills, discipline, and a sense of identity. It carried me across states, into gyms I never thought I'd enter, and connected me with people who shaped who I am today. Yet, as much as the game gave me, it also mirrored back the parts of myself I didn't fully understand.

Reflecting on my playing days, I see parallels everywhere, between the player I was and the therapist I am now. By sitting with my childhood experiences, I can now recognize how life off the court shaped how I showed up on it. The way I carried myself, the preparation I brought to practice, even my attitude during games— all of it traced back to home.

Growing up in the early 2000s with a single mom and two older brothers shaped me in complex ways. There was love, resilience, and toughness, but also challenges that lingered long past my youth. Layer onto that the weight of societal messages about what it means to be a Black man, and the struggle deepened. I remember vividly believing the lie that "boys don't cry." I learned to see emotions as weakness, and on the court, that belief translated into conflict. Coaches saw me as a kid with an attitude problem. What they didn't see was the pain beneath the surface.

Therapist-me knows better now. Every behavior points to an unmet need. Back then, I was told what to do and how to act, but no one asked why I was acting that way. Basketball became my only outlet. A place to release frustration, anger, and grief. But instead of receiving tools or coping strategies, the focus stayed on my "bad behavior." I wasn't seen; I was managed.

Years later, when I stepped into the other jersey, the therapist's, I realized how powerful certain frameworks would have been for me as a player. Acceptance and Commitment Therapy (ACT) is one I return to often. At its core, ACT is about psychological flexibility: staying true to your values while learning to adapt your thoughts and behaviors in the face of ever-changing circumstances. For athletes, this is the essence of the "next play mindset." You miss a shot, turn the ball over, hear your coach yelling from the sideline, you don't let it dictate the rest of your game. Outsiders can spot when an athlete is stuck, spiraling after one mistake. Mental toughness gets praised, but ACT provides the roadmap.

Two processes within ACT stand out most: present-moment awareness and self-as-context. Being present sounds simple, but as a player, I struggled with it. One or two mistakes could ruin my performance because I'd carry them with me, possession after possession. I wasn't playing the game in front of me; I was stuck in the one behind me.

Self-as-context is about knowing who you are at your core, regardless of thoughts or emotions. Feelings and setbacks are temporary; they don't define you. That understanding would have freed me from the weeds of negativity, allowing me to reset and move forward.

Working with these concepts post-sport has not only helped me reflect but also equipped me to guide others who are walking similar paths. And if I could distill what therapy means to me now, I wouldn't describe it as a hierarchy of therapist and client. I see it as a partnership. I don't want my clients to view me as "the expert" but as a teammate. Together, we're chasing the same goal—growth, healing, clarity.

The old phrase still holds: T.E.A.M. Together Everyone Achieves More. I may not wear a uniform anymore, but I'm still the same player. The jersey has changed, the role has evolved, and the game looks different, but the mission is the same. Through lived experience and education, I've discovered more about my own core needs while helping others discover theirs.

CHAPTER 8

FROM APPLAUSE TO ALIGNMENT

The world doesn't warn you about what happens after the buzzer.

Everybody wants to talk about the grind to get there: the two-a-days, the flights, the moments when your body screams "quit" but you keep going anyway. But almost nobody talks about the silence that follows. And for a lot of athletes, especially those hooping overseas, that silence is heavy.

It's the weight of homesickness. The mental toll of chasing contracts in unfamiliar countries. And sometimes even guilt—for being the one who "made it."

About a year ago, I wrote an article on this after a late-night call with one of my overseas guys. What started as a vent session turned into a reflection on something I had seen but rarely heard discussed: survivor's remorse.

Here's what I wrote:

...

"For every trophy lift and confetti shower, there are unspoken truths lurking just beneath the surface of postseason play. For many professional athletes, especially those competing overseas, success comes with a silent weight: survivor's remorse.

We tend to celebrate the glory of winning seasons while overlooking the complex emotional toll that follows. The guilt, isolation, and post-season lows are real. And if you ask many overseas athletes, their biggest challenge isn't just the physical grind or adapting to a new culture, it's navigating the disconnect between public perception and private experience.

Survivor's remorse in athletes often mirrors what psychologists have observed in other high-performance settings. It's that nagging question: Why me? Why did I get the opportunity, the contract, the moment on the big stage, while friends or teammates were left behind?

Lynette Hughes and Gerard Leavey linked this emotional conflict to identity disruption and social guilt. Athletes who have "made it" can feel torn between celebrating their success and mourning the struggles of those they came up with. This tension becomes especially visible during the postseason, when social media highlights wins while privately, many athletes wrestle with feeling undeserving or alone.

For overseas players, isolation hits differently. Living thousands of miles from home, often in countries where the language, food, and daily customs are unfamiliar, adds a layer of emotional fatigue that rarely gets talked about. Add in a winning season or deep playoff run, and the isolation can intensify. You're expected to be locked in and grateful, but that doesn't erase the homesickness or the pressure to perform.

What makes it harder is the misconception that playing professionally overseas is some kind of extended vacation. Family and friends may assume your life is luxurious, filled with travel, sightseeing, and leisure. But the reality is far from that. The days are structured, the stakes are high, and the margin for error is slim. One bad game can cost you your next contract.

Once the season ends, the emotional hangover begins. Athletes go from structured routines, performance goals, and adrenaline highs to... nothing. That sudden silence can be deafening. According to research from Wylleman and Lavallee (2004), transitions out of competitive play, even temporarily, can trigger mood disruptions, loss of identity, and difficulty adjusting to "normal life."

Overseas players face this on a different scale. Many return home only to be met with outdated understandings of who they are or what they've been through. They aren't the same people who left, but the world around them expects them to fit right back in. That misalignment leads to feelings of jealousy (from others), resentment (within the athlete), and sometimes a deep sense of loneliness.

Survivor's remorse isn't weakness. It's HUMAN. It's a signal that athletes are not immune to the emotional complexity of their journeys, no matter how polished the highlight reel looks. Mental performance professionals, coaches, and support networks need to better understand how these feelings show up and offer safe spaces for athletes to unpack them.

For those of us working in this space, it's not just about enhancing focus or mental toughness. It's about reminding athletes that feeling conflicted after success is normal. That it's okay to honor your wins and acknowledge the cost.

Especially for overseas hoopers grinding through long seasons away from home, just know, what you're feeling is valid. You're not alone. And your story, in all its messy, layered beauty, MATTERS."

...

I didn't realize at the time how much this would resonate. Players from all over reached out. Some thanking me for saying what they couldn't, others admitting it was the first time they felt seen.

And if you're reading this now, maybe it resonates with you too. Maybe you've felt that pull, the mix of gratitude and guilt, of being proud you made it and wishing your people could've come with you.

That's what being human in this game feels like.

Because at the end of the day, this journey isn't just about how many trophies you stack up. It's about learning how to carry the weight of winning without letting it crush your soul.

There's a quiet shift that happens when you get tired of performing for the applause. When the grind starts to feel hollow. When you realize all the effort, all the pain, wasn't always for you. It was to prove something. To *someone*. Maybe a parent, a coach, a crowd that's no longer watching.

That's the danger of chasing approval. It's addicting but never fulfilling. You always need more. Another contract. Another shoutout. Another viral moment. But the peace? It never lands.

Purpose is different.

Purpose doesn't show up only when you're winning. Purpose doesn't disappear when your minutes drop. It doesn't shrink under pressure or inflate with praise.

Purpose says, "Even if nobody claps, I know why I'm here."

And that's the heart of this whole section. Learning to shift from *doing for approval* to *living from purpose*. From grinding to impress to growing with intention.

I had a pro client tell me not long ago, "Man, I don't even know if I still want this, or if I'm just scared to let go of what everyone else expects of me." That's real. That's what happens when your identity gets hijacked by the game. When you've spent so long being what people needed you to be, you forget who you really are.

So, how do you come back to center?

You get grounded. You get honest. And you get spiritual, not necessarily religious, but tapped into something bigger than stats and storylines.

Faith is a big one. Not just in a higher power, but in your higher purpose. In yourself. In what's been placed on your life that no scoreboard can measure.

When I help athletes navigate this shift, we slow everything down. Strip it back to core values. Who are you when no one's watching? What matters to you off the court? What impact do you want to have, not just in the game, but in the lives of those around you?

We build inner routines around that. Things like spiritual check-ins. Breathwork. Journaling. Prayer.

Stillness. Whatever centers you in truth.

One player I work with starts every day by writing three reminders: *Play free. Play real. Play loved.* That's alignment. That's the mental game.

Because when you're aligned with your purpose, you're dangerous, in the best way. You don't play scared. You don't chase validation. You move with clarity, confidence, and freedom.

And that kind of presence is contagious. When you live from purpose, other people feel it. They might not be able to explain it, but they'll know there's something different about you. Something grounded. Something real.

That's soul work. And that's why this chapter sits at the center of the book.

Everything before this was about sharpening your mind. What's coming next? That's about strengthening your spirit.

Because when the noise fades, when the crowd leaves, when the jersey gets folded up for the last time, *this* is what remains:

Your character. Your values. Your heart. Not what you did for approval, but how you lived with purpose.

And that matters more than anything.

Approval might get you applause. But purpose? Purpose will give you peace.

...

SURVIVOR'S REMORSE – MEMOIR BY JASON BURNELL

The Guilt That Follows Success

It's real.

I remember during my second year playing overseas, these waves of emotions and thoughts started hitting me. Back in my freshman year of college, I came in as part of a highly recruited class. People said we were one of the best groups to ever step on campus. But out of all of us, I was the one who didn't start... barely even played. There were nights when my name sat in the box score with a big fat DNP next to it. I can still see the walk-ons getting subbed in before me, right in front of my parents. That kind of embarrassment sticks with you.

It eventually pushed me to transfer. I went from being a Division I disappointment to a JUCO grinder fighting for another shot. Fast forward a few years, and there I was, a professional, having achieved a level of success I'd never imagined. Yet early in my career, I wrestled with this haunting question: Why me?

It felt like the guys I came in with deserved it more. There were times I didn't even look like I belonged in the same gym as them. They would embarrass me in every drill, every king-of-the-court game, and every scrimmage.

But then something clicked.

My dad used to say it all the time growing up: "The cream always rises to the top. You might have to stir it up a little, but the cream always rises." That stuck with me.

I finally rose to the top. And my success is nothing to feel guilty about.

I worked too damn hard for this. I was the one grinding at 4 AM airport shifts. I was the one logging hours and hours in the gym. I'm the one who went toe-to-toe with first-round draft picks and held my own. Nobody can take that from me, so why would I take it away from myself by feeling guilty?

Don't apologize for your success. Don't shrink yourself to make others comfortable. God doesn't make mistakes, and the work you do in the dark will always shine in the light. Remember this: Purpose over pressure. The timing is never wrong when it's God's timing.

Isolation in the Midst of Success

I learned early on that people who live the "ball is

life" lifestyle are something else. Not regular. Honestly, a little crazy. That's just how it is.

You don't just stumble into this life. You have to love this shit.

Moving halfway, or all the way, across the world is just part of the sacrifice. And the faster you accept that wherever you're playing is home, the better. Back home? That's not home anymore.

It's not easy. For some, it takes years to adjust. It took me until year four to really figure it out.

Here's what I learned: make yourself at home. Build a routine. Blend the culture you came from with the one you're living in. Sometimes it'll cost you, financially or emotionally, but it's worth it. I even started finding my own apartments outside the free ones that teams provide. Ten months is a long time to come home every day to a place that feels temporary.

When it comes to food, all you need is three good restaurants and a handful of meals you can rotate. Don't fight the culture, embrace it. Don't expect people to understand you. You're in their country. At least try to learn the language.

And when people back home act like you're on some extended vacation, shift your language. Tell them you're "heading to work" instead of "going to practice." That subtle shift changes how they see what you do.

This isn't a vacation, it's your livelihood.

But here's the thing: it's okay to isolate yourself. Just don't let yourself feel lonely. There's a difference. Keep the main thing the main thing, your career. And whenever homesickness hits, return to your why. Remember why you started and why you're still here.

Purpose over pressure.

Postseason Lulls and Emotional Crashes

This one? This one is tough.

The smallest things can trigger it. Nothing hits harder than landing back home, calling your usual guy, and hearing, "Nah, I don't sell anymore."

All jokes aside, coming home after a long season can feel... weird. You've just spent 10 months on a six-day workweek, one day off. Now suddenly you're in vacation mode, and it doesn't feel the same.

Everything that happened while you were gone comes crashing in: losses, breakups, even the silence from people who disappeared when you refused to send them money. Overseas feels like a false reality. No matter how much life happens back home, you're too far away to do anything about it.

I know that feeling. I went through it in the middle of my best season ever. I got a call one Wednesday: my grandmother was dying. On her deathbed, she asked me, "Baby boy, when are you coming home?"

She was my heart. My whole world.

I flew home the next day to say goodbye, then flew back two days later to play in a game.

After two weeks, I flew home again to bury her. I can still see the casket lowering into the ground, and it felt like my entire soul went down with it.

Thirty-seven days after that, my closest uncle passed. I got the news in a club after a big win. Emotionally, I was lost.

But the expectation never changes. You still have to perform. You still have to show up.

It's like being in the middle of a game, playing well, when the ref stops everything because you're bleeding. You have no idea where the blood is coming from, and you're pissed off because you don't want to come out. They clean you up and send you back in. But later in the shower, you feel the sting from a tiny cut you didn't even know existed.

That's what grieving felt like for me. A slow bleed nobody could see.

And I bled all over the people I loved most. My wife, especially. She was there for me in my darkest chapter, and I poured all my pain onto her.

I couldn't grieve like everyone else. There was no time. I didn't even fully process my uncle's death until his birthday two months later. The next day, I completely crashed during a playoff game.

I pulled myself together, but I knew when I got home for the offseason, the real emotional test was waiting.

That being said, there's no perfect recipe for life. What works for me might not work for you. I tried it all... trips with the guys, throwing huge parties, chasing distractions. None of it worked.

Eventually, I learned what I needed: to get back to work. Ball is life. It grounds me.

Find what keeps you sane in the offseason. Lock it in and do it every year.

Love yourself. Be patient with your journey. It's okay for your path to have purpose. Just don't let it become pressure. Pressure kills the joy. Purpose breathes life back into it.

And remember: If you keep looking back, you're bound to trip moving forward.

MORE THAN A GAME

WHEN THE BALL STOPS BOUNCING

You don't stop being an athlete, you just learn to compete in a different arena.

The crowd's roar fades. The final buzzer hits, and for the first time in years, there's no next play to draw up, no practice to lock in for tomorrow, no offseason grind waiting to pull you back in. Instead, it's just you... and this quiet question that won't leave your mind: *So... what now?*

It's a moment every athlete will eventually face, but nobody really prepares for it. The identity that pushed you through your toughest wins and gut-wrenching losses, the version of you that felt untouchable in uniform, it starts to slip away. And for the first time, you're forced to ask yourself: *Who am I without the game?*

For me, that question started forming long before the final buzzer. It was layered into my college years, hidden beneath the surface of every practice and every game.

Over my four-year career, I had 42 different teammates. And this was before new rules let college athletes switch schools more easily or make money from sponsorships, that now make constant roster turnover normal. Back then, that kind of roster change was rare. But as the point guard, I had to adjust at the start of every year. Learning personalities, play styles, and comfort zones on and off the court. Was I perfect at it? Hell no. But it was part of the job if I wanted any chance at success.

It wasn't a role I sought out or even wanted. It was placed on the shoulders of a 19-year-old kid who moved across the country chasing a dream. So much of my energy went into understanding everyone else. Building chemistry, holding it all together. So much, that I never had a moment to figure out who I was outside the game.

When you're in it, you don't realize how much of yourself you're giving away. You show up every day thinking about how to make it work for the team, how to earn the coach's trust, how to make sure your teammates are comfortable and focused on the goal. The game doesn't ask for part of you, it demands all of you. And as a competitor, you give it willingly because that's what greatness requires. That's the price of wanting to be the best. And I know this applies both on and off the court. We apply ourselves fully when we're invested on an emotional level. When we want something so bad we're willing to lose parts of ourselves if it means nearing the edge of what we're capable of.

But there's another side to it, a side most people don't see. Underneath the highlight reels, the box scores, and the celebratory photos, there's this quiet, constant pressure. It's the weight of expectations, yours and everyone else's. It's the mental checklist running through your head at night when you can't sleep: *Did I lead well enough today? Did I say the right thing in the huddle? Am I doing enough to prove I belong here?* You learn to push it down, to keep moving. There's no time to pause when the schedule won't let you breathe.

And then, before you know it, the clock runs out.

I remember sitting in the locker room after my final game. Shoes undone. Jersey drenched in sweat and something heavier. I wasn't crying like I thought I would. I wasn't even as sad as I'd imagined. I just felt... empty. For years, my life had been mapped out by quarters and halves, practices and bus rides, film sessions and team huddles. It gave me purpose. It gave me direction. And now? Now there were no more scouting reports, no more pregame routines, no more "next season." Just silence.

That silence is deafening because athletes aren't taught how to prepare for it. From the time we're kids, we're wired to chase the next thing, the next game, the next accolade, the next level. The identity of "athlete" becomes more than a label; it becomes our foundation. It's how we're introduced, how people see us, and how we see ourselves. But no one tells you what happens when that foundation cracks.

When the final horn screams, it's like stepping off a cliff. Everything you've known, your routine, your purpose, your validation, disappears in an instant. And you're left trying to figure out where you land.

For me, that landing wasn't graceful. I stumbled. I questioned everything. Who was I without the game? What value did I bring if I wasn't scoring, leading, or wearing the jersey? I didn't have answers, and for a while, that scared me. Even to this day, there are still moments where these questions continue to resurface.

But as the days turned into weeks, I realized something: the game didn't define all of me. It shaped me, sure. There were parts of me that would always be intertwined in the lines of the court. The game taught me discipline, focus, and resilience. It showed me what it meant to sacrifice for something bigger than myself. And even though my playing days were over, those lessons didn't disappear. They were still in me. I just had to learn how to use them differently.

That's the part no one tells you about, the pivot. It's not about replacing the game; it's about rediscovering yourself beyond it. The same fire you brought to the court, field, or track can fuel something new. But you have to give yourself permission to step back, reflect, and rebuild.

Looking back, I know I wasn't perfect. Not in how I handled things or how I moved. But there's value in the effort. There's something to be said for trying to make something out of nothing. That experience left me with lessons I can now share, so maybe someone out there learns to manage the pressure, the stress, and gives themselves the chance to explore life beyond the surface.

To every athlete reading this: the end of your career isn't the end of you. It is the beginning of something different. I won't tell you it is easy. There will be days when you miss the game so much it aches deep in your chest. There will be moments when you question your worth and wonder what comes next. I remember those first weeks after my last college game. The silence was the loudest thing in the room. No scouting reports waiting for me, no 6 a.m. lifts to drag myself out of bed for, no locker room noise to drown out the doubt. At the first family gathering, someone asked me, "So what's next?" and I realized I didn't know how to answer without starting with "I'm a basketball player." That unraveling was painful, but it was also real.

Years later, I stood in front of a room full of current athletes at the Black Student–Athlete Summit in Chicago, and everything came full circle. I told them what I wish someone had told me back then. I spoke about the Final Redshirt, the pause after your last season where you are forced to reflect, recalibrate, and figure out who you are when the jersey no longer does the talking. I spoke about navigating graduate school as a former athlete and the weight of battling imposter syndrome while carrying cultural expectations into spaces where you feel out of place. And I spoke about the importance of amplifying your voice, especially as a Black student-athlete, because silence might keep you comfortable for a while, but it will not carry you forward.

That day, while looking into the eyes of athletes who were still in the middle of their grind, I realized something about myself. Every concept I shared wasn't just a lecture, it was my life. I had lived through the Final Redshirt. I had walked into graduate classrooms unsure whether I belonged. I had felt the tension of holding back my voice in spaces that didn't always reflect me. Speaking those truths out loud gave me one of the clearest moments of purpose I've ever had. I understood that when the ball stops bouncing, the story doesn't end, it shifts. The same lessons the game taught me about discipline, resilience, and identity were the ones I now carried into every room I stepped into.

That room reminded me of something I had to learn the hard way. The unraveling of your identity is not the end of your story. It is the beginning of another one.

But trust me when I say this, you are more than your stats, your jersey, or your accolades.

You don't lose your greatness when the lights go

out. You don't lose your passion when the crowds stop cheering. You just have to learn to channel it in a new way.

Take a deep breath. Honor the version of you that gave it everything. And know that this isn't where your story ends. It's just where the next chapter begins. And this time, you get to write it on your terms.

Maybe this is the moment to let yourself pause. To step away from the grind you've known for so long and create space to breathe, reflect, and rebuild. Just like you trusted the process as an athlete, this transition requires its own process—one that's less about pushing forward and more about sitting still long enough to figure out who you are without the jersey.

Think of this stage as the "gap year" of the athlete's journey. Just like students take time to travel, reflect, and recalibrate between school and career, athletes need that same space to rediscover themselves beyond their sport. Too often, we overlook the power of a pause, mistaking it for weakness instead of what it truly is… wisdom.

In college athletics, a redshirt year is viewed as an opportunity. It's a chance to develop, to train, to prepare for what's next without the pressure of performing. But what if we applied this concept to life after sport? What if athletes could give themselves permission to step back, reflect, and rediscover who they are when the jersey is no longer their defining marker? This is what I call The Final Redshirt, a season dedicated to rebuilding, not rushing.

There is strong evidence that intentional reflection and recalibration can benefit individuals in transition. Research in positive psychology emphasizes the importance of self-reflection and meaning-making during life changes. Many athletes who step away from competition experience identity loss, which can later present itself as emotional fatigue, lack of purpose, or even depression in some. However, when this transition is approached with intention and purpose, it can become a season of growth and self-discovery rather than one of loss.

Studies on transitional periods, like gap years, show long-term benefits for students and professionals alike. A 2015 study found that individuals who took gap years reported higher levels of adaptability, self-awareness, and life satisfaction. These same benefits can translate to former athletes who allow themselves time to process the shift away from sport. By reframing this transition as an opportunity instead of an ending, athletes can begin to envision their lives as multidimensional rather than defined by a single role.

Athletic identity, how much you define yourself by your role as an athlete, isn't a bad thing. Honestly, it's part of what makes you great. It fuels your focus, discipline, and confidence. It's the reason you've been able to push through tough moments and perform at a high level. But here's the thing: when your entire identity is wrapped up in the game, the moment it ends can hit harder than any loss you've ever faced.

When athletes tie their sense of self only to their sport, the end of a career can bring a wave of psychological challenges. Things like feeling lost, anxious, and even numb. And it makes sense. I mean, most of us never had the time or space to figure out who we were outside the game. The grind, the routine, the culture, it demands all of you and leaves no time for self-reflection. It asks you to go all in, leaving almost no room for other sides of yourself to grow. That's why this transition feels so heavy. It's not just the game you're leaving behind; it's the version of you that's been center stage for so long. And when the other parts of yourself are under-established, having had little time in the spotlight, you end up feeling lost and empty.

But this doesn't mean you're broken. It means you're evolving. You're stepping into a version of yourself that can integrate the athlete within you into new roles, relationships, and contributions. The Final Redshirt is your chance to make this evolution intentional.

This pause is about doing the inner work that was often pushed aside in the name of competition. It's about asking questions like:

- *What do I value most?*

- *Where have I felt alive outside of sport?*

- *What kind of person do I want to become in this next chapter?*

Tools like mindfulness and journaling can help you slow down and unpack the questions that have been sitting in the back of your mind. Research backs this up, these practices can help you regulate emotions, process the highs and lows, and reconnect with a sense of purpose. And listen, expanding your circle matters too. Seek out mentors, therapists, or career coaches who can pour into you during this season. Let them remind you that you don't have to figure this all out on your own. Asking for help isn't weakness, it's strength.

Another big shift? Redefining your routine. For years, your habits were wired for performance—morning lifts, recovery sessions, film study, scouting reports. Now it's time to create new rhythms rooted in growth, self-care, and curiosity. Instead of waking up for early-morning workouts, maybe you wake up to journal or meditate. Instead of team meetings, maybe you spend time networking or exploring a creative outlet you never had time for. These small changes begin rewiring your mind for a bigger, fuller definition of success.

And then there's your inner voice. That voice matters. Replace "I used to be…" with "I'm becoming…" You're not erasing your past self. **You're building on it**.

You're taking everything the game taught you: discipline, focus, resilience, and now, applying it in new spaces.

Identity doesn't exist in a vacuum. As a Black male athlete, I know firsthand how cultural narratives shaped my understanding of success. Growing up, the message was always "keep grinding" or "don't let them see you struggle." Vulnerability wasn't modeled, and stepping back felt like failure. But I've learned the truth: giving yourself space to evolve isn't quitting, it's healing.

As a father, a consultant, and a former college athlete, I've come to understand that we carry multiple identities. The key is learning how to weave them together in a way that feels real, not forced. You don't have to abandon the athlete within you. You just have to teach that part of yourself how to exist in new arenas.

You don't stop being an athlete, you just learn to compete in a different arena.

Some of the most successful athletes I know aren't chasing clout or contracts anymore. They're leading businesses, mentoring youth, building families, and making an impact in ways that can't be measured on a scoreboard. They didn't stop being athletes, they just started competing differently.

Winning doesn't look like stats anymore. It looks like a purpose. Impact. Contribution. It's about waking up knowing your life holds value beyond what you did on the court, field, or track.

So, take this time. Honor the athlete you were. But don't stop there. Begin the work of becoming the person you're meant to be.

This isn't the end of your story. This is the start of your second season.

And in this season, the game hits differently. It's not about chasing trophies anymore, it's about chasing wholeness.

💬 **Reflection Prompt:** What are three qualities you developed as an athlete that you can carry with you into this next season of life?

LEGACY OVER LIKES

I've learned that some of the most critical parts of growth happen when nobody's watching. We live in an era where success feels tied to visibility. Followers. Likes. Comments. Metrics that suggest you matter. But here's what I've seen, over and over again: the loudest voices aren't always the ones doing the deepest work. And the ones making the biggest difference often don't get applause until much later, if ever.

This isn't just something I believe. It's something I've lived.

"Just because they don't see you yet doesn't mean you aren't built for impact, quality doesn't rush recognition."

I keep coming back to this quote. In a world where visibility often feels like the currency of success, it's easy to feel overlooked when your name isn't trending, your work isn't reposted, or your presence isn't instantly validated. But here's the truth: visibility isn't the same as value. And being seen isn't the same as being built for impact.

Some of the most influential moments in my life, and in the lives of the athletes and professionals I've worked with, came in the shadows. Quiet reps in empty gyms. Deep conversations that never made it out of a private conversation. Decisions to stay disciplined when no one was watching. If you're in a season where it feels like your effort isn't being acknowledged, I want you to know this: your identity is not defined by applause. It's shaped by alignment. Alignment with your values, your purpose, and the long game you're playing.

We live in a culture that rewards speed and spectacle. But real identity? It's forged in patience, resilience, and consistency. That's how presence gets built. That's how legacy takes root. Whether you're an athlete developing your voice, a leader carving out space in your industry, or a creator putting your soul into your craft, know that just because they don't see you yet, it doesn't mean you aren't already making an impact.

I learned this in a way that hit me hard. A few summers back, a clip of close friend got traction. One of those quick, clean moments that plays well on a screen. His phone buzzed all night. DMs, reposts, people hyping it like it was everything. And he explained that for the first hour, it felt good. But by the time his head hit the pillow, he felt empty. I knew what the camera didn't catch: the earlier session that day where he sat in a hallway with a younger teammate and talked him through a confidence spiral. No camera. No clip. Just a kid who needed steadiness in a moment that could've broken him. The viral moment fed the algorithm. The hallway moment fed a soul. That moment taught me something I won't forget—likes give you a rush; legacy gives you roots.

Flip the scene. Another game, different year, but this time for me. Box score didn't love me. No gaudy numbers, nothing that would end up in a highlight montage. Afterward, a teammate grabbed me and said, "We don't win without you." It wasn't flattery—he listed the screens, the communication, the calm when it got shaky, the huddle where I looked a freshman in the eye and told him he was ready. No cameras. No clip. But I slept like a rock that night. That's the difference.

Likes are fast, flashy, external, and fading. Legacy is slow, grounded, internal, and lasting. Likes are the mixtape dunks, loud, viral, gone when the algorithm shifts. Legacy is the charge you take in the fourth quarter nobody's saving that to their story, but it flips the game. Likes are fireworks. Legacy is a lighthouse. One explodes; the other endures.

The spotlight is sexy and seductive, but it fades. Legacy doesn't. And when you're building for legacy, you realize you're not in a race to be seen. You're in a process to become undeniable. So let them scroll past. Let the noise be loud. You're not here for likes. You're here to leave something that lasts.

Legacy isn't about the number of trophies you've collected, the followers you've gained, or the applause that echoes in arenas. It's about the invisible threads you weave into the lives of others, the impact that lingers long after you're gone. When the crowd stops cheering and the bright lights fade, what remains isn't the external validation but the way you've chosen to pour into the people and spaces around you. In today's world, it's easy to confuse influence with impact. Social media makes it seem like likes equal value and followers mean leadership. But deep down, you know true leadership isn't about popularity, it's about responsibility. Leadership, at its core, is about elevating others. It's about making people around you better, not just for a season but for life.

I think of a guard I worked with who was obsessed with clips. Every film session turned into, "Can we cut that for IG?" He wasn't selfish; he was wired to believe visibility equals value. Meanwhile, the guy who set the tone in practice: diving on the floor, directing traffic, dapping up teammates after blown plays, barely posted at all. Two years later, guess which name comes up when I visit that locker room? Not the one with the followers. The one who changed how people felt about themselves when they were around him.

Another athlete with a quiet presence couldn't care less about the algorithm. He started bringing a teammate to every extra workout. Not to show off, but to show how. He didn't trend. He transformed. Ask the staff there who their culture shifted around, and they'll tell you his name without blinking.

This lesson shows up in coaching, too. Think about Coach Mike Krzyzewski from Duke University. His career wasn't just about the wins and championships, though he collected plenty (if you are a UNC fan, pshh). It was about the people he developed along the way. Coach K didn't just coach basketball; he coached character. He poured into his players as young men first, athletes second. He taught leadership, teamwork, and accountability in ways that stuck with them long after they left Cameron Indoor Stadium. His legacy isn't limited to banners hanging in the rafters. It lives on in the lives of his former players, leaders, fathers, mentors who carry his lessons into locker rooms, boardrooms, and living rooms across the world, The Brotherhood. Grant Hill once said about Coach K, "He didn't just prepare me for basketball. He prepared me for life. He taught me how to lead, how to work with people, and how to stay true to my values even when it wasn't easy." That's the ripple effect of a leader who plays the long game.

Now, consider Deion Sanders. A cultural icon both on and off the field, Deion's legacy is different from Coach K's but just as powerful. As a player, his confidence and swag changed the way people thought about cornerbacks. But it's his work as a coach that's redefining legacy for a new generation. At Jackson State and now at Colorado, Coach Prime isn't just building programs; he's building men. He preaches discipline, faith, and self-belief in a way that resonates with players raised in a culture of instant gratification. He tells his players, "If you look good, you feel good. If you feel good, you play good. If you play good, they pay good." But beneath the charisma is a deep commitment to teaching young athletes how to handle adversity, how to be accountable, and how to take ownership of their futures. His legacy isn't about proving doubters wrong. It's about proving to his players that they can be leaders in their families and communities long after their playing days are over. He's showing them how to shine without losing their soul.

Then there's Stephen Curry. Steph doesn't command the room with sheer size or volume; he leads through humility, work ethic, and consistency. He revolutionized basketball with his shooting, but his legacy isn't just about changing the game, it's about changing lives. Steph is known for his quiet confidence and his ability to lead without needing to dominate. He celebrates his teammates' success as much as his own. He's intentional about his faith, his family, and using his platform to give back. On and off the court, he models what it means to live in alignment with your values. When the Warriors were struggling during rebuilding years, Steph stayed the course. He trusted the process, uplifted his younger teammates, and set an example of what perseverance looks like. That's transformational leadership in action. Bringing out the best in others by believing in them even before they believe in themselves.

All this proves something simple but not easy: building a legacy starts with character. It's doing the right thing when no one's watching. It's leading with integrity, humility, and service. Leaders who serve others first, rather than chasing power, create lasting change. They're not worried about being the center of attention. They're focused on building people up, not themselves. When you prioritize relationships and value people, you inspire trust and loyalty that outlast any single achievement. You understand that greatness isn't about standing above others. It's about lifting them higher.

Legacy is about transformation. Transformational leaders push those around them to think differently, grow in confidence, and chase greatness. They hold the vision high and challenge their people to rise to it. They don't settle for average because they know what's possible when someone feels seen, supported, and inspired. Like Coach Prime, they combine high expectations with high levels of care. Like Steph Curry, they model faith and steadiness through adversity. That mix of standard and support creates a culture where greatness becomes the expectation, not the exception.

Still, no one leadership style works in every moment. The best leaders know how to adapt based on the needs of their people. Sometimes you need to step in and teach the fundamentals. Other times, you coach alongside your people, pushing them to think for themselves. And sometimes the best thing you can do is step back and let them take the lead. Great leaders don't have one gear; they know when to switch it up. It's not about control. It's about stewardship. And stewardship builds trust—the foundation of any legacy worth leaving.

This isn't only for athletes. Parents and coaches, you shape this too. When adults feed the "likes" machine, living through a kid's stat line, breaking down a game in the parking lot, only praising outcomes, you wire athletes to chase applause. When you nurture legacy by praising effort, honoring composure, and modeling humility you wire athletes to build character.

One athlete told me he dreaded the car ride home more than the fourth quarter. Another told me the sentence that changed his life was, "I love watching you play." Same sport. Different soundtrack. The soundtrack you provide becomes the story they tell themselves. If you want to raise leaders, celebrate the behaviors that build them: communication, courage, accountability, grace under fire. That's legacy work, and you're in the front row.

Here's the truth: legacy isn't built in a day. It's built brick by brick in the choices you make when no one's watching. It's found in mentoring someone without expecting credit, serving others even when it's inconvenient, and staying aligned with your values even when it costs you something. Likes fade. Legacy doesn't. When you commit to giving more than you take, you create a ripple effect you may never fully see, but others will feel. That's the impact. That's the kind of influence that doesn't just trend for a week. It echoes for generations.

And so, the challenge is this: ten years from now, nobody will remember your likes. But they'll remember how you made them feel. They'll remember who you became when the gym was empty and the lights were off. They'll remember the way you lifted a room that didn't have enough air in it. So, what are you choosing to build?

Write your own definition of "Unapologetic Athlete." Start one small daily practice that brings you alignment. Tell one person your story, the honest version, and ask for nothing in return. Plant a seed you may never see grow. Then plant another.

Because this isn't about arriving. It's about returning to who you are when no one's watching. It's about choosing legacy over likes, substance over spectacle, roots over fireworks. I'm still choosing, too. Some days I get it right. Some days I get humbled. But the question I come back to never changes: am I building something that lasts?

Your turn. The next chapter is already in motion. Written in your reps, your relationships, your quiet decisions.

Leave the ending open.

Step into it.

And let the work speak...

FOR THE NEXT GENERATION

Let's pause for a second and break the fourth wall. Let's remove any barrier still standing between author and reader. This chapter's going to flow a little differently. It's broken into three parts: one for parents, one for coaches, and one for athletes. You can read straight through or skip to the section that speaks to you most. I'm not here to waste your time, so take what you need and dive in.

[FOR PARENTS]

Sports can be one of the greatest teachers in life. They teach discipline, teamwork, and resilience. They show kids what it means to push through when things get hard and what it feels like to win and lose with grace. But here's the truth: as much as sports can build someone up, they can also break someone down if we're not careful, especially when the voices outside of the game get louder than the ones within.

As parents, you hold one of the most powerful roles in your child's athletic journey. You are the first coach they'll ever have, the first cheerleader in their stands, and sometimes, unknowingly, the first critic in their ear. And I say that not to call you out, but to call you in. Because your influence doesn't stop at drop-offs and post-game snacks. It's in the way you talk about their performance on the car ride home. It's in the energy you bring to the sidelines. It's in how you help them process tough losses and how you celebrate their small wins.

If you want to help your child thrive, not just as an athlete but as a human being, you have to create space for them to be unapologetically who they are. That's the sweet spot where hustle meets heart. That's where the magic happens. I've worked with countless athletes who've told me their sport stopped feeling like their thing somewhere along the way. It became about living up to expectations, making parents proud, or proving doubters wrong. And when that happens, the joy that drew them to the game in the first place starts to fade.

Your job isn't to push them harder, it's to help them love harder. Love the game, love the grind, and most importantly, love themselves through it all. That means separating your dreams from theirs. Maybe you didn't make varsity. Maybe you wish you had gone further in your sport. But this isn't about rewriting your story through them. It's about helping them write their own.

And before we go further, let's normalize something. It's hard being a parent in this space. You love your kid, you want the best for them, and yet there's no manual for how to balance pushing them toward their potential and protecting their joy. Some days you'll feel like you were too hard on them. Other days you'll wish you had said more. That push-and-pull is normal. Every single parent of an athlete wrestles with this balance. You're not alone in the tension of wanting them to be tough but not crushed, challenged but not burned out. That conflict isn't a flaw, it's proof you care.

I've seen parents beat themselves up for being "too much" or "not enough." Let me ease some of that guilt: every parent I've ever met has wrestled with those same questions. You are not supposed to get this perfect. What matters most isn't perfection, it's connection. And when you aim for connection instead of control, you help your child hold onto the joy that brought them to the game in the first place.

Of course, encouragement is powerful, but parents often need something even more practical—real tools they can use in the heat of the moment. One of the simplest but most impactful is language. Words matter. The difference between, "Did you win?" and "How did you feel about your effort today?" is massive. The first ties your child's value to a result. The second ties it to their experience and growth. Instead of, "Why didn't you score more?" try, "What did you learn from that game?" Those small swaps change how your child sees themselves.

Another tool I swear by is the 24-hour rule. One of the toughest things for kids is getting into the car after a game, already replaying mistakes in their head, and hearing their parents immediately break it all down. I know the urge comes from a good place. You want to help, you want to guide, but often, it does more harm than good. Try waiting until the next day. Let emotions settle. A calm conversation after 24 hours usually goes further than any "instant analysis."

And then there are the check-ins. Kids don't always want a lecture. Sometimes they don't even want advice. Try asking, "Do you want me to just listen, or do you want advice?" That one question gives them power. It tells them you respect their voice in their journey. It's a game-changer because it takes you out of "fix-it" mode and puts you into "support" mode.

Don't overlook the invisible wins. Did your child keep fighting even when they were tired? Did they support a teammate even though their own game wasn't great? Did they bounce back after a mistake? Celebrate that. Stats don't tell the full story of a game, but the way they show up, their effort, their resilience—that's where the real growth happens.

And here's the bigger picture that I don't want you to miss. At some point, the jersey comes off. The lights dim. The game ends. And who are they then? The athletes who navigate that transition the best are the ones who've always known they're more than their sport. They've been reminded again and again that their identity doesn't hinge on performance. And parents, you play the biggest role in making sure that's true.

When your child learns resilience after a tough game, that resilience doesn't stop when they leave the gym. It shows up when they face a hard exam, a tough job interview, or even a personal setback later in life. The lessons they take from sports are practice for the rest of their lives. You're not just raising athletes, you're raising future leaders, teammates, parents, and community members. Every time you model humility, gratitude, or balance, you plant seeds they'll carry into every other space they walk into.

That's the legacy. Not legacy in the sense of trophies on a shelf, but legacy in the sense of raising whole, grounded, resilient human beings who carry lessons from the game into the rest of their lives.

Sometimes the best way to do that is to slow down and ask yourself a few questions. Am I celebrating effort as much as results? Do I leave room for my child's voice in their journey? How can I show up as their parent, not their coach, this week? Do I give my child space to rest and recover, or do I only value their grind? What message do my actions send about what matters most?

The point of these questions isn't to create guilt, it's to create awareness. Awareness is what turns impulse into intention. And intention is what helps you consistently show up as the parent your child needs most.

Because at the end of the day, hustle is great. Discipline is great. But hustle without heart leads to burnout. Heart without hustle leaves potential untapped. The goal isn't to push your child until they break or to let them drift without direction. It's to help them find that place in between. The place where hard work meets passion, where ambition doesn't crush joy.

You can help them get there by celebrating their effort over their stats, making it clear that your pride isn't conditional. Normalize rest. Let them know it's okay to take a break... to breathe, to recover. Encourage self-expression and let them show up fully as themselves, quirks and all. Be their safe space. No matter what happens on the field or court, they need to know your love doesn't change. Live it yourself. Show them what balance looks like in your own life.

When you do this, you're not just raising an athlete. You're raising a confident, resilient, and authentic human being. And trust me, whether they go pro, play in college, or hang up their sneakers after high school, that's the kind of win that matters most.

You have the power to make sports one of the greatest gifts in your child's life. Not because of trophies or scholarships, but because of the person they become through it all. So as you guide them, remind yourself: your job isn't to mold a perfect athlete. It's to nurture a whole person. Help them find where hustle meets heart. And watch them flourish, on and off the field.

Affirmation: *I am raising a child whose worth goes beyond the scoreboard. My role is to help them chase their passion with heart, balance, and courage.*

[FOR COACHES]

I was once told by a former supervisor, "Coaches are the real sport psychologists." That sat with me. I didn't agree right away, but I couldn't shake the truth behind it either. Because whether they realize it or not, coaches are shaping minds as much as they shape bodies. Every film session, every sprint rep, every sideline talk, there's a message being delivered, and most of the time, it's about way more than the game.

And coaches, here's the real weight of that: You're the gatekeepers. You can build athletes who love the game, or kids who break under it.

Let that breathe for a second.

That line came up during a podcast I did not too long ago. We weren't talking stats, schemes, or game strategy, we were talking about soul work. About what it means to lead the next generation of athletes into their truth, not just into a system. About how the influence of a coach can either open doors or close them shut before a kid even figures out who they are.

See, the best coaches don't just teach the game. They teach athletes how to be unapologetic in who they are on the court, in the classroom, at home, wherever. They give them the space to ask real questions, to have real emotions, and still push hard. They allow exploration but don't let kids coast. They push in multiple directions, but they pour in deeply along the way.

And that's the part we forget: you can't pour from an empty place. If you're going to call out greatness in a young person, you better be doing the work to see them clearly, because identity isn't built in silence. It's built in how we speak to these athletes when the lights aren't on. It's built in those tough car rides after a bad game, or the moments when you choose not to bench them for a mistake, but sit with them and ask, "What happened out there?" not with judgment, but with curiosity.

I'm not saying coaches should be therapists or take on a role that's bigger and heavier than they signed up for. There's a line that shouldn't be crossed, a boundary that should remain in place to some extent. There are things you might not be trained to handle, and that's okay. That's why there's a lane for licensed sport psychs, mental performance coaches, counselors, and all the professionals who've spent years studying this. But what I am saying is this: If you're coaching, you're already in the mental game. Whether you like it or not. Whether you know it or not.

And so, I stand in that middle ground now. I don't fully agree with the idea that coaches are the only sport psychs, but I absolutely believe they're the first ones. The first line. The front door. The gatekeepers.

So, what are you guarding?

What are you letting in?

What are you keeping out?

Too many young athletes are falling apart because no one's creating space for them to just be human. To fail and still be worthy. To win and not feel defined by it. To love the game without being consumed by it. And that's where coaching has to evolve.

Here's what I hope coaches take from this:

- **Encourage movement in multiple lanes.** Don't box your athletes in. If a kid wants to play soccer and learn music and start a YouTube channel, let them. Help them chase it all and hold them accountable to doing it with excellence.

- **Create psychological safety without softness.** There's a difference between making space and making excuses. Speak truth but speak it from a place of belief. Correct without cutting.

- **Collaborate with mental professionals.** You're not expected to do it all. But you should know when something's above your pay grade. Build bridges with sport psychs, mentors, and therapists. Your athletes deserve that network.

- **Pour in. Then pour again.** Don't just coach the skill, coach the soul. Teach your athletes how to reset, how to breathe, how to reflect, and how to name what they feel.

- **Remind them they are more than the jersey.** Talk about legacy. About values. About identity when the lights go off. Plant seeds early that their worth isn't tied to box scores or followers.

That's what helps build athletes who show up in this world with purpose, not just performance. Athletes who are unapologetic in the best way. Who know who they are, even when the scoreboard says otherwise.

And if you're reading this as a coach, just know, we see you. You matter. You're shaping futures. And the best ones? They build people first and let the game follow.

[FOR ATHLETE]

As we've discussed in all the earlier chapters, there's a quiet strength in owning your voice. It's not about being the loudest in the room or saying the most, it's about saying what's real to you, even when it feels heavy. It's about standing firm in who you are and letting that shine through in every space you walk into. Too many of us have learned how to shrink. We've mastered the art of keeping the peace, blending in, and holding back because somewhere along the way, we were taught that our words didn't matter. But holding your tongue doesn't protect your peace, it slowly chips away at it.

You have to know this: your voice carries weight. Your story deserves space. And the world doesn't need another watered-down version of you. It needs the real you. Unfiltered. Unapologetic.

Right now, you might be standing at a crossroads. One path feels safe—it's the familiar silence, the comfort of not risking too much. The other path? That's where your power lives. That's where you step out, speak up, and own every piece of who you are. It won't always be easy. Fear will whisper reasons to stay quiet. Doubt will try to convince you that no one cares. But hear this: your silence doesn't serve you. It doesn't serve your purpose. And it sure doesn't serve the people you're meant to impact.

James Baldwin said it best: "Not everything that is faced can be changed. But nothing can be changed until it is faced." Using your voice isn't about making noise for the sake of it, it's about setting yourself free. It's reclaiming your narrative and deciding that no one else gets to write your story but you.

Courage doesn't always look like standing on a stage or leading a movement. Sometimes, it's speaking up in a meeting. It's telling someone how you really feel. It's being brave enough to say "this is who I am" without flinching. Every time you choose to honor your voice, you're building strength. You're showing yourself that you matter.

Start with the little things. The words you speak to yourself. The conversations you've avoided. The truths you've been scared to admit out loud. Write them down. Say them in the mirror. Share them with someone you trust. Every time you speak your truth, your voice gets louder, and not just to the world, but to yourself.

And while you're at it, take stock of who's in your corner. Surround yourself with people who encourage you to be real. People who don't flinch when you show up fully. The right circle will remind you of your worth when you forget and challenge you to grow when you get too comfortable.

So, how do you amplify your voice? You just start. Even if it feels messy. Even if it shakes. Even if your words come out softer than you wanted them to. Because every time you speak, you're taking a stand for yourself.

You don't need permission. You don't need validation. You already have what you need, you just have to believe it.

As Audre Lorde said, "When I dare to be powerful, to use my strength in the service of my vision, then it becomes less and less important whether I am afraid."

This is your call: stand in your power. Speak your truth. Show the world that your voice isn't just meant to be heard, it's meant to echo.

So, I'll ask you this: What will you do with your voice now?

...

LESSONS BEYOND THE GAME – MEMOIR BY DEONTRE BROWN

As a college athlete, basketball taught me plenty about the sport, but it taught me even more about myself.

On the basketball side, the first lesson was simple: the work is never done. Coming out of the suburbs of Illinois, I was "the guy." I had all the accolades I wanted from a high school career, and I thought those achievements would carry me straight into college success. But when I got to college, reality checked me quick. By my sophomore year, I ran into my teammate who was actually better than me.

That realization stung. I wasn't used to being second best. At first, I felt nothing but animosity, jealousy, and even hate. But after getting torched in practice for a few weeks, I stopped sulking and started paying attention. I watched how he worked. He was relentless. Running at 5 a.m. before conditioning, shooting before and after practice, showing up on nights when everyone else was out partying. His consistency was on another level.

That's when it clicked: I thought I was working hard, but he was outworking a hard worker. I realized I had taken my foot off the gas, like earning a scholarship was the finish line. In that moment, the jealousy disappeared, replaced with admiration. I set a new standard for myself. In my head, he was Jordan, and I was Kobe... and we all know how that story goes. From him, I learned you can never relax. The work never stops.

My dad's voice echoed those same lessons during workouts: "There's a kid in Chicago that's not tired, not missing, and he's going to kill you if you play like that!" That stuck with me. No matter how hard you think you're working, someone else is working harder. So, I decided to work like I was paranoid. Always chasing, never satisfied.

The second lesson I learned was about authenticity.

Looking back, I know my college career could have been better if I had simply trusted myself. Too often, I played not to mess up, trying to be exactly what the coach wanted instead of playing my game. That hesitation turned into overthinking, which turned into mistakes, which usually landed me on the bench. But on the nights I finally said "forget it" and just played like the version of me that earned a scholarship in the first place, I played my best games. That's when I stood out. That's when I thrived. Consistency was my problem, but the lesson was clear: you have to be yourself, no matter who's on the court, no matter who's coaching you.

As a skills and development trainer, I carried that forward. I learned that every player is different. Some need encouragement, others need you to get on them, and some just need a reminder of why they grind. My job became finding each player's pressure point and coaching them in the way they respond best.

The final, and maybe most important, lesson came from one of my clients. I've trained NBA players and celebrities, but one of the most impactful conversations I ever had was with a rapper. He told me about the grind before he blew up. Dropping a song every week, showing up at the studio even on the days he didn't want to. He admitted that most of those days, nothing happened. But after 55 weeks of consistent work, he showed up on one of those "don't feel like it" days, and made the song that changed his life.

That hit me hard. His message was clear: the days you don't want to show up are the days you need to show up. That's when the breakthrough often comes. The lesson is to fall in love with the process, because the results are born from showing up daily. Whether it's getting extra shots, eating right, lifting, or just refusing to quit.

From him I took two truths: never give up, and fall in love with the process. You never know which day will be the one that changes everything.

To the next generation, I say this: discipline will set you apart. The game will still be there in five years, the parties will still be there when you graduate, and the relationships will always be there. But opportunities won't wait. Go after what you want with everything you've got, and don't stop. Tomorrow isn't promised.

And always remember.

Stay UNGUARDABLE.

129

PART IV

SOUL WORK

CHAPTER 12

FAITH & FLOW

The court is empty this morning. Not the kind of empty that feels lonely, more like the kind that feels honest. The air is still, the faint hum of the building just enough to remind me the world is awake while this space stays quiet. My steps echo once, twice, then dissolve into the rafters. I didn't bring a ball. I'm not here to shoot. I'm here to think, to breathe, to listen for what gets drowned out when the gym is loud. Sometimes you need the absence of noise to hear the truth.

I'm standing on the three-point line like it's a border between two countries... what I know and what I'm still learning. Most of my life has been about crossing lines like this, painted or invisible. Lines between training and burnout, between confidence and ego, between the image people see and the person I'm actually becoming. Right now, the biggest line in front of me is the one between belief and faith. I can feel it under my feet. I can feel myself balancing on it.

We don't talk about that line enough in sports. We pump the idea of believing in yourself like it's the ultimate trophy. Say it enough times and it becomes your reality. But belief has edges. It's tied to evidence. It asks for proof. You believe because you've done it before, because your film looks clean, because the drills were sharp, because the numbers say this should go your way.

Faith is different. Faith does not care about evidence. Let clarify something: Faith is not religion. Religion is structured: texts, traditions, community. Faith walks into the gym the morning after you were humbled and says, "I'm still here." Faith stands beside you when you're not trending, when your minutes are thin, when the plan you wrote in ink gets smudged by life. Belief can get you started, but faith is what keeps you standing when the floor starts to shake, and it will shake.

Belief will always want a receipt. It says, "I believe I can hit this free throw because I've made it a thousand times before." Faith says, "I'm taking this shot like I've already made it, even if I've missed the last ten." Belief hunts for patterns to validate itself. Faith chooses a direction without needing a guarantee. If your belief is built entirely on results, then every bad game chisels away at your foundation. Your confidence starts negotiating with your fear: Maybe you're not who you thought. Maybe this moment is too big. Maybe it's time to play smaller.

I'm not interested in negotiating with fear. Faith doesn't negotiate. Faith doesn't care about the scoreboard. Faith plays the long game in a short-term world that equates worth with today's box score. And here's the part you might not want to hear: If you've only built belief, the first real storm will break you. If you've built faith, every setback becomes another line in the story you're still writing, another rep in a strength you can't see yet.

Pause with me, right here. Breathe. Ask yourself and answer out loud so you can hear it: *Do I live more in belief or in faith? If the results stopped showing up for a while, would my effort look the same? When no one is clapping, am I still all-in?* If your chest tightens reading that, good. Don't flinch. Let it tighten. That tension is where the truth sits. That's soul work.

A world-renown mental skills coach said it to me best, you can hold both, belief and faith, but the order matters. Belief should be powered by faith, not the other way around. If belief goes first, you're only as strong as your last performance. If faith goes first, you're anchored to something that can't be stolen by one bad week.

This is where flow glides into the conversation, almost like it heard its name. Flow is that sweet spot where your mind, body, and spirit move together like they've been rehearsing in secret for years. The game feels unforced. Time is elastic. Noise fades. The rim looks big. You can't muscle your way into that zone. You can only let go enough to be carried there. Faith is letting go. It frees you from obsessing over the outcome so you can immerse yourself in the process. When I say release, I'm not saying you should stop caring. I'm saying you need to learn to trust your preparation so deeply that you stop bargaining with the moment.

In flow, you aren't calculating shooting percentage or rehearsing excuses. You aren't managing other people's perceptions in real time. You are here. You are answering the possession in front of you with your full attention. Presence is faith in motion. Presence says, "I don't need a guarantee to give everything."

Every competitor I've known carries two voices. Belief's voice is the hype man: "You've got this. You've done it before. Stay smooth." Faith's voice is quieter and deeper: "Even if you've never done this before, you still can. Even if they doubt you, move like you belong." Belief's voice gets loud when you're on a roll. Faith's voice waits for the moment you actually need it. The missed shot, the turnover, the coach's side-eye, the contract conversation that goes sideways. In those moments, belief alone is brittle. Faith has roots.

Faith can live inside religion, but it doesn't have to. Faith is the internal decision to commit to something bigger than your comfort: God, purpose, the future you're building, a calling you can't shake. I'm not here to tell you what to believe in. I'm here to ask why you're willing to stand in the fire. If you don't have that *why*, pressure will find the soft spots and widen them.

You can be unapologetic without ever stepping into a church, mosque, or temple. But you cannot be an unapologetic athlete without faith. Without it, the first honest hit life throws will fold you in half. It's only a matter of time.

Think back to the last transition you faced. New team. Role shift. Injury. End of a season. A door closing you thought would swing open forever. Belief says, "I've been here before; I'll figure it out." Faith says, even if I haven't been here, I will grow into what's next." If your identity is glued to what you do today, belief collapses when that "today" ends. Faith says, "My worth isn't rented from my stat line. My value doesn't expire when the jersey does. My purpose refuses to be confined to a single chapter."

Try this right now. Yes, right now. Pull out your phone or notebook. Write three moments when belief failed you, when the proof wasn't there. Label what you reached for in each moment. Did you reach for people? Rituals? Words? Silence? That's the root system of your faith. See it on the page. Don't pretty it up. The truth isn't fragile.

And when faith grows, the grind changes shape. Without faith, the grind is punishment, a debt you're trying to pay off to feel worthy. With faith, the grind is preparation, a gift you give your future self.

When I was younger, I thought the grind meant more. More hours, more reps, more sweat. And sometimes it does. But the grind without faith is just motion. Faith gives it direction. It transforms conditioning from punishment into capacity. It turns lifting into training for the mental load you'll carry when the game gets ugly and life gets real. Faith is the architecture; effort is the bricks. Without architecture, bricks are just a pile and nothing more.

I didn't always understand that. My mom used to force me to write down what she called "three positivities" every single day. At the time, I hated it. I'd roll my eyes, scribble something half-assed just to get it over with, and think, *What does this even have to do with basketball?* To me, it felt like busywork—something soft that had no place in the hard grind I thought mattered most. I pushed back, sometimes even refused, because I couldn't see the point. But she didn't let up.

Day after day, she held me accountable. Slowly, something shifted. What started as three empty lines on a page began to feel like three anchors. I started noticing little wins I would've ignored. I started catching myself leaning into belief instead of doubt. Back then, I didn't have the language for it. I wasn't in this field yet, but those "positivities" were reps. Quiet, unseen reps of faith that were reshaping the way I saw myself and the game.

So, we train faith like we train skill. Reps of trust. Reps of showing up without guarantees. Reps of staying with the process when the results are slow or invisible. Reps of choosing values over vibes. If that sounds abstract, keep reading.

Let's get practical. I want you to build anchors, small, repeatable cues that return you to the present under pressure. Start with breath. Inhale through the nose for four, hold for two, exhale for six. Feel the air exit. Again. Two more. That's not just calming your nerves; it's sharpening perception. Next, eyes. Pick a physical point before every rep. A logo on the floor, the back of the rim, a seam on the ball, and let your gaze soften around it. That single point gives your nervous system a target. Now, feet. Ground both feet before every decision. A micro-pause. It takes half a second and buys you clarity. Finally, language. Choose a cue that isn't about the outcome. Not "make it." Try "through" or "trust", or "finish." One word. One beat. Repeat it when your brain tries to sprint ahead.

Think of these anchors as agreements. Each one says, "I will return to what I can control." You aren't hoping to be confident; you're training the conditions that allow confidence to find you.

Let me put on the mentor hat and hand you a drill I use myself. Call it Uncertainty Reps. Once a week, do one controlled thing without a guaranteed payoff. It might be reaching out to a coach you admire with a thoughtful note, shooting your shot on an opportunity you feel "almost" ready for, or practicing a new skill publicly instead of in secret. The goal isn't the *yes*. The goal is to prove to yourself that you can act faithfully without a contract from the future. After each rep, journal two lines: *What I feared. What actually happened?* Read those lines back to yourself before your next rep. Your nervous system is trainable. You just have to put in the work.

Here's a quick hypothetical to ground this. I'm talking with a veteran coach I trust... been around decades, coached across continents, nothing dazzles him anymore. He tells me, quietly, that what kept him centered wasn't superstition; it was structure: morning silence before the handset lights up, a short gratitude line sent to one person on his staff daily, three non-negotiable minutes of breath before the team steps on court, and a commitment to leave one conversation better than he found it. He says that in the worst weeks where injuries piled, the media is loud, roster questions—those simple acts kept him from swinging wildly with each result. "I didn't pray for wins," he laughs, "I prayed for presence." That sticks with me because it's honest. Presence is the doorway. Wins are what pass through when your house is in order.

Transitions test everything. The end of a season. The offseason nobody sees. The injury that turns momentum into stillness. The city you move to without your circle. In those spaces, people try to outsource their ground: new identities, new noise, new distractions. You'll be tempted to grab anything that promises certainty. Don't. Build certainty from the inside out. Identity before role. Values before validation. Direction before speed. If you need a measuring stick, ask: *If this were taken away tomorrow, would I still respect how I moved today?* If the answer is yes, you're doing it right. If the answer is no, adjust now. Not in a week. Now.

Tonight, give yourself a 20-minute audit. In the first five minutes, write what you have faith in, not what sounds good but what's real. In the next five, write where you're pretending belief is faith, where you only act brave when the odds are stacked in your favor. Then, for another five minutes, write your one-sentence purpose in this season. Not your life. This season. And for the final five minutes, list three actions you'll take this week that align with that sentence, and one thing you'll stop doing because it betrays that sentence. That's an alignment drill, not a vibes exercise. Tape it to your wall. Read it before you scroll.

Let's talk science without killing the soul of it. Flow emerges when challenge and skill match closely, when your goals are clear, when feedback is immediate, and when you have enough attention left over to adapt. Faith helps you step into a challenge that's slightly above comfort because you aren't auditioning for safety. Faith keeps you from shrinking your goals to protect your ego. Faith sharpens feedback because you stop taking every data point personally. And faith frees attention because you're not trying to control a thousand variables that never belonged to you. That's why faith and flow feel like cousins. They both require presence, and they both reject panic.

There's a mental skill here that matters: acceptance. Not passive, not giving up, active acceptance of what is, so you can respond to what can be. Without acceptance, you fight reality and waste energy. With acceptance, you collect reality like a scout collects information. Faith gives acceptance backbone. You can accept hard truths because they don't define your worth. You can make bold adjustments because you aren't trying to protect an image. When I work with this in myself, I use a three-step loop: name the truth, choose the value, take the next right action. Example:

- Truth—I'm tense and rushing.

- Value—Composure.

- Next action—Exhale, ground feet, single cue, go.

I don't need to feel perfect to act aligned. That's faith, too.

Another tool is implementation intentions. These are if-then agreements that pre-decide your behavior under stress. If I miss two in a row, then I touch my chest, breathe out, say "through," and attack the next rep with pace. If I catch myself scanning for approval, then I refocus on my breath and the next task cue. If practice gets disrupted, then I shorten and sharpen: one drill, one focus, one standard. This is integrity in motion. You are rehearsing faith so thoroughly that when the moment arrives, you don't ask who you are, you demonstrate it.

Where does ambition fit in? Right beside faith. I'm not asking you to mute your hunger. I'm asking you to align it. Ambition without faith becomes addiction to outcomes. Ambition with faith becomes devotion to craft. One drains you when you don't get what you want. The other develops you regardless of the day's result. Ask yourself: *Do I want to be admired or to be aligned?* One is a moving target. The other is a daily practice.

Here's a 21-day Faith & Flow cycle to test in real life. Day 1–7, Mornings: three minutes of stillness before your phone, write one sentence of purpose for the day, and identify a single process goal you can fully control. Workouts: set one anchor (breath, gaze, foot), one cue word, and one measurable standard you'll hold regardless of outcome. Midday: ninety seconds of reset—inhale four, hold two, exhale six, repeat, then ask: What's my job in the next hour? Evenings: two-line debrief. What did I do that aligned with purpose? What will I repeat tomorrow? Day 8–14, add one Uncertainty Rep each day: small, deliberate actions without guaranteed payoff. Track the fear you felt and the reality that occurred. Day 15–21, introduce a No-Outcome Block: choose one practice session or workout where you refuse to check metrics until the end. Stay fully with the task. After, reflect on attention quality and how it felt to execute without constant judgment. Throughout all 21 days, hold one Service Rep per week: do something that benefits someone else's development with no public credit. Why? Because faith matures when it's not all about you.

I want you to hear me clearly: Stop outsourcing your grounding to other people's reactions. Stop waiting for perfect conditions to go all-in. Stop treating your confidence like a lease that the world can terminate. Decide who you are and act like it long enough that your nervous system believes you. You don't fake it until you make it; you faith it while you build it. There's a difference.

Plant your feet where you are. Yes, actually do it. Unclench your jaw. Drop your shoulders. Inhale through your nose to four, hold two, exhale to six. Again. Notice three sounds around you. Name silently what you're grateful for in this exact moment, something small you would miss if it were gone. Touch your sternum with your palm and say quietly, "Here." That word is a promise. You're telling yourself where your life happens. Not in memory. Not in fantasy. Here.

Now for the part most people skip: Write a letter to yourself dated ninety days from now. One page. Describe how you moved with faith over those three months. Be specific in what anchors you used, what risks you took, what you released. Seal it and set a reminder to open it. Then do the work that earns the letter.

One more mirror. Three yes-or-no questions that decide the arc of your season: *Am I willing to do small things consistently without applause? Am I willing to be seen trying things I might not be great at yet? Am I willing to keep my word to myself when convenience argues against it?* If you have two yeses and a maybe, you're close. If you have three yeses, you're already moving differently than most.

I'm thinking about the athletes and individuals who will read this and feel both called out and called forward.

Good. That's the point. I'm not here to coddle your talent or sugarcoat the truth. I'm here to coach something more. I can't carry your work for you, and I won't pretend you can bypass the struggle. But I can help guide you and, more importantly, be honest with you: You are capable of more steadiness than you believe, and the path to it isn't mystical. It's laced in choices. It's rooted in training faith like a skill until it becomes your default under pressure.

If your mind is arguing with you right now... But what if I fail? But what if they laugh? invite those questions in like background noise and keep moving. Faith doesn't delete doubt. It refuses to be directed by it. You can carry doubt in your backpack and still climb.

Take this with you: When belief fades, as it sometimes will, faith can hold you without drama. Faith steadies your hands, steadies your breath, steadies your choices. Faith keeps you from trying to control what was never yours to hold and puts your focus back where your power lives: the present moment, the next right action, the person you're becoming.

Some will cheer for you. Some will root against you. None of them can do your work for you. None of them can hand you peace. But you can. You can walk into rooms with a quiet fire that doesn't ask permission. You can choose anchors over anxieties, process over panic, and integrity over image. You can ground your ambition in faith so that, whether the path is straight or wild, you are not easily moved.

So tonight, when the lights go down and your phone finally stops buzzing, ask yourself three closing questions and answer them with your whole chest: *What is my faith anchored to, specifically, not vaguely? What am I willing to do daily that proves that the anchor is real? What will I refuse to do anymore because it betrays that anchor?* Write it. Sign it. Live it.

And if you need a sentence to carry in your pocket when the day turns heavy, carry this one: Faith doesn't make the grind easier, it makes it worth it.

Read it again when the noise spikes, when the doubt creeps, when the plan bends. Then breathe, ground, choose your cue, and move.

The rest will meet yo8u at the pace of your presence.

CHAPTER 13

SHARPENING THE INVISIBLE EDGE

The alarm hasn't gone off yet, but the room is already alive in its own way, the low hum of the heater, the faint street noise, the softness of a day that hasn't made its demands. The first mental rep can live here. One slow inhale through the nose, a short hold, and a long, controlled exhale until your shoulders drop and your jaw releases. This is claiming control. That decision, made before the world even knocks, sets the tone for everything that follows. It's the kind of decision that may feel small, almost invisible, but like a seed planted in darkness, its effects grow with time and repetition.

Across every level of sport, one truth holds: The mind isn't a passenger, it's the engine. It decides how much of your skill actually arrives under the lights. Bodies get trained in plain view; minds get sharpened in the quiet margins. Ignore those margins and you'll find out too late that potential without preparation is just a guess. Mental reps aren't optional, they're the line between almost and undeniable, between moments you control and moments that control you.

Athletes who make mental work non-negotiable bring a different nervous system into battle. Their heart rate still jumps, but their focus stays sharp. They hear the noise without surrendering the wheel. They recover from mistakes in seconds because they refuse to let errors define them. Science calls it attentional control, cognitive reappraisal, interoceptive awareness, psychological flexibility. On game day, it's poise, composure, and the uncanny sense that time bends in their favor.

Daily mental reps like breathwork, visualization, affirmations, gratitude aren't just mood boosters. They change brain chemistry, rewire neural pathways, and reshape how you respond under stress. Breath slows the heart and steadies the decision-maker inside you. Visualization primes your brain for high-pressure execution, so moments feel familiar before they happen. Affirmations align identity with action. Gratitude trains your perception to notice opportunities instead of obsessing over obstacles.

Think about what happens when you've rehearsed a skill so many times that you can perform it under fatigue, distraction, or doubt. That's what these reps do for the mind. You're no longer fighting yourself in the moment, you've already walked this path so often that your mental steps land without hesitation. You've built a familiarity with pressure that turns it from an enemy into a signal: it's time to rise.

When practiced consistently, these reps deliver compound returns. Confidence isn't left to chance; it's manufactured through repetition. Reaction times shrink. Recovery from mental errors becomes faster. Decision-making sharpens under fatigue. Athletes who master these subtleties step inside the pressure of it all. Precision under fire isn't luck; it's rehearsed. And in the moments that define careers, that rehearsal shows.

Implementation intentions, those if–then blueprints turn reactions into reflexes. If tension creeps in after a mistake, then exhale, plant your feet, speak your cue, and move. If you catch yourself searching the crowd for validation, then lock your eyes on an anchor and get back to work. Done often enough, these patterns become automatic, freeing up mental bandwidth for strategy and execution.

There's no one-size-fits-all. Your reps should fit your sport, schedule, and style. A sprinter's mental routine will differ from a goalkeeper's, but the principle is the same: you don't wait for the perfect moment; you instead prepare for imperfect ones. The determined athlete trains so their performance holds when conditions don't. Whether it's the silence of a pre-dawn run or the chaos of an away-game crowd, their mental reps are the tether to their best self.

Quick resets are gold in competition. A bad play doesn't spiral into a bad game when you can turn chaos into clarity. You miss. Heat rises. Instead of spiraling, you hit your sequence: focus point, slow exhale, cue word, go. Most people watching from the sidelines can't see this ability but it's obvious to those who compete against you, it's what separates the good and the great. It's the quiet edge that tilts the game in your favor without a single stat recording it.

Over a season, mental reps become an insurance policy. Fatigue muddies concentration. Stress turns small mistakes into big ones. Breath and language shift your mindset from feeling threatened to feeling challenged, helping you stay calm and perform. They also sustain motivation, keeping effort consistent regardless of scoreboard swings. In a long season, when physical energy dips, it's these mental habits that keep you playing at a high level.

Athletes who commit to mental reps also build resilience against slumps. Instead of chasing form, they return to fundamentals that restore it. Instead of hoping confidence returns, they create the conditions that generate it. In this way, mental reps are not only a performance enhancer but a career extender. They allow you to perform at a high level longer, and with less mental wear and tear.

Small moments add up. The rep you do when nobody's looking matters just as much as the one you do in the heat of competition. Breathing while tying your shoes. A quick visualization in the locker room. Choosing a cue word instead of a curse after a mistake. These aren't glamorous, but they accumulate like quiet deposits in a bank account you'll draw on when it matters.

And mental reps don't just prepare you for the high points, they keep you from breaking in the low ones. Sports are unpredictable. Weather changes. Calls don't go your way. Opponents come in better prepared than expected. The mental habits you've built become the scaffolding that holds you upright when external circumstances try to shake you.

It's important to remember that mental reps are not confined to traditional "quiet time" practices. They can be woven into the way you walk onto the court, the way you take a free throw, the way you shake hands with an opponent. These are micro-opportunities to reinforce the mindset you want to live in. Every routine, every breath, every thought is either training your focus or training your distraction.

5 Daily Mindset Drills for Athletes

- *Four-Six Breathing: Inhale for four counts, hold two, exhale for six; two to five minutes to lock in or reset.*

- *Targeted Visualization: Five minutes of realistic scenarios, rehearsing the best responses.*

- *Identity Affirmations: Three provable statements, each matched with an action.*

- *Three-Line Gratitude: Nightly, name three moments worth carrying forward.*

- *One-Minute Reset: Focus point, slow exhale, cue word, immediate action.*

A lot of people see this kind of mental work as fluff that fills their valuable time, but this is far from that. This is about building a core you can trust when the ground shifts. Athletes with patterns stay anchored; those without go searching for steadiness in the wrong places. These five drills are the anchors you can return to in the storm.

Research on choking under pressure shows how self-focus can sabotage performance. Mental reps protect automatic skills and keep execution clean. Challenge-threat theory proves that perceived resources change how you meet the moment. Daily reps increase those resources. Acceptance-based strategies teach you to act on values even with discomfort breathing down your neck. Over time, these approaches condition you to embrace rather than avoid the high-stakes moments.

Pair reps with existing triggers: Breathe when you sit up, visualize after you lace up, repeat affirmations before the first drill, practice gratitude before lights out, and reset after mistakes. By linking them to routines you already have, they become effortless to maintain. You remove the friction that makes new habits fail.

If you're serious about unapologetic living as an athlete, think about the environments that challenge you most: hostile crowds, long travel days, unexpected changes in game plans. Then engineer your mental reps to match those challenges. The goal is not comfort; the goal is capability. You want to be able to walk into the most chaotic environment and find the same steadiness you have in your quietest moments.

Run a seven-day trial. Start with two drills, add another midweek, and refine. By the end, measure your focus, recovery speed, and composure. Keep what amplifies you. Drop what doesn't. The routine should be portable and durable, able to travel with you and hold under the weight of pressure. Like a trusted piece of equipment, it should feel strange to compete without it.

Mental reps aren't a softer path; they're the sharper one. They demand honesty and consistency. You can bluff in the weight room. You can't bluff in the three breaths after a turnover. The version of you that shows up there is the one that earns trust from teammates and fear from opponents. Build that version on purpose. Make your habits so sharp that when pressure shows up, it's walking into your arena.

When the day closes, the same choice that started it is still yours: control over reaction, calm in chaos, trust in the repetition you've invested in. Mental reps don't make the grind lighter; they make you unshakable inside it. They create a version of you that not only survives the hardest moments but thrives in them, turning preparation into performance and performance into a legacy. And that's not something that happens by chance, it's the result of every intentional rep you've stacked, day after day, long before the lights came on.

UNAPOLOGETIC ATHLETE

I want you to stop for a second.

Not skim. Not multitask. Just pause.

And listen to that voice in your head.

You know the one. The one that's been running commentary all day. The one that spoke up when you hit snooze this morning. The one who whispered when you walked into that room earlier. The one that told you you're either ready... or not.

Now let me ask you this: do you trust that voice? Does it push you forward, or does it hold you back? Does it sound like a coach or a critic?

Here's the truth: talks with that voice are the most powerful conversations you will ever have. And whether you realize it or not, you are always listening. If you want to change how you perform in sports, in business, in life, you've got to start with how you speak to yourself.

I'm not just saying this because it sounds good. Research in the psychological sciences backs it up: your self-talk shapes your motivation, your focus, even your ability to stay calm when the game's on the line. But let's put the research aside for a second. Let's talk about you.

Think back to a moment where it all came down to you, a big game, a career-defining meeting, a conversation that could shift your life. What was running through your mind? Did you walk in saying, "I'm built for this"... or did doubt creep in, whispering, "What if I'm not enough?"

Here's what you need to know: your body will follow the story you tell it. Step up to the free-throw line, the podium, the opportunity, saying, "I always rise to the occasion," and your mind and body will respond in kind. Walk in thinking, "I don't belong here"... and your actions will reflect that story, too.

This isn't just about mindset. It's about identity. Identity isn't built when the cameras are on. It's built in the shadows. One conversation at a time.

Growing up in the Bay, and still to this day, I see this everywhere, athletes grinding in empty gyms, entrepreneurs betting on themselves with no guarantees. And one thing became clear to me: belief alone isn't enough. You can't just say you're ready. You have to become it.

So here's my challenge to you: what's the story you've been telling yourself lately? Is it one that moves you forward, or one that keeps you small? If you're ready to stop performing for likes and start building for legacy, you're in the right place.

And that's where this begins: owning your moment isn't about waiting for the perfect conditions. If this book has shown you anything, it's that the conditions will rarely be perfect, and that's not a disadvantage, that's an opportunity. The storms, the missed calls, the nights you didn't think you had it in you... they're all reps. They're proof that you can keep showing up even when it isn't convenient or comfortable.

Think about it. Those challenges you've faced, the ones that tested you the most, were also the moments that shaped you. They taught you to trust yourself in uncertainty. They showed you that you can find strength in discomfort, that you can adapt when the plan changes, and that you can still move forward when the ground beneath you feels shaky. Perfect conditions aren't where greatness is built; greatness is built when you show up in imperfect conditions and still find a way to make it work.

We've talked about mental reps. Those daily, intentional drills that sharpen your focus, strengthen your composure, and train your mind to see solutions where others see problems. They aren't flashy. No one's cheering for you while you visualize, breathe, journal, or reset your perspective after a setback. But that's the point. The moments no one sees are the exact moments that decide everything. They're the quiet investments that compound into confidence when the lights are on and the pressure is high.

We've talked about resilience, not the fake kind that ignores pain and pretends nothing's wrong, but the real kind that faces the hard truth, adjusts, and still chooses to move forward. Real resilience isn't about never feeling doubt or frustration; it's about feeling those things and refusing to let them dictate your outcome. That's what separates performers from passengers. Performers face adversity and respond with intention. Passengers let adversity decide for them.

We've talked about emotional control, how to keep your head when the scoreboard, the crowd, or your own doubts try to pull you off track. That control doesn't make you cold or detached; it makes you consistent. It means you can perform at your highest level regardless of the noise around you. In the moments where emotions run hot, emotional control is the skill that keeps you locked into your mission instead of getting pulled into the chaos.

We've talked about faith, not just in the spiritual sense, but in your preparation, your values, and your process. Faith is what holds you steady when the results aren't instant and the road feels endless. It's the belief that every rep, every sacrifice, and every lesson is building something, even if you can't see it yet. Faith is trusting that the seeds you've planted will grow, even on the days you feel stuck in the dirt.

We've talked about identity, how to know who you are when the game ends, when the title changes, when the applause fades. Because if your identity is only built on what you do, it can be taken away. But if it's rooted in who you are, it becomes unshakable. Identity is the foundation that keeps you standing when circumstances shift. It's what allows you to reinvent, rebuild, and still feel whole.

And we've talked about legacy, choosing to measure your life not by how many eyes are on you, but by how many lives you impact. The scoreboard might show the numbers, but the real win is knowing you played your game with integrity, passion, and purpose. Legacy is about leaving something behind that outlives the final whistle, the last sale, or the closing curtain.

The truth is, the unapologetic athlete, whether on the court, in the office, or in life, doesn't wait for permission. They create the moment. They walk into spaces with clarity about who they are and refuse to shrink, even when the room feels unfamiliar. They don't adjust their worth to fit the room; they adjust the room to fit their worth.

And yet, here's where I stand now: even after writing this, even after all the work, I'm still figuring it out. I've gained clarity, yes, but the answers keep unfolding. Who am I beyond the game? I'm still answering that question every day. I'm still learning, growing, experimenting, failing, adjusting. And that's not a weakness, it's part of the journey.

If there's one thing I've learned, it's that identity is more than performance. Confidence is built brick by brick, not overnight. And faith and flow matter just as much as grind and hustle. These are lessons I carry with me, but they're not just mine; they're universal truths that you can claim, too.

At the same time, I don't pretend to have it all figured out. I wrestle with questions just like you do. How do I balance ambition with peace? How do I detach my worth from results when the world still feels scoreboard-driven? How do I stay grounded when expectations, my own and others', keep rising? These are the questions I carry, and I'll be honest: I don't always have clean answers. But maybe that's the point. Being unapologetic isn't about knowing everything; it's about being willing to sit with the questions and keep moving anyway.

So, let me turn it to you: what questions are you carrying right now? Where are you still wrestling, still searching, still unsure? Because this book was never about me giving you the perfect blueprint. It was about giving you tools, stories, and affirmations you could use as you walk your own path. Your path will look different from mine, but you're not walking it alone.

That's why I want to leave you with an invitation, not a conclusion. Don't close this book like it's finished, open it like it's a door. Write your own definition of what it means to be an unapologetic athlete. Start one small daily practice that brings you into alignment with who you want to be. Share your story with someone else who needs it, because you will never know who needs it until you tell it. Whatever it looks like, take one step forward.

Because I'm still figuring this out, too. And maybe that's the point... This journey isn't about arriving. It's about staying open, staying honest, and staying unapologetic.

So, when that voice in your head speaks up tomorrow, when it tries to push you forward or pull you back, don't just listen. Lead it. Shape it. Own it. And remind yourself: this is your moment. Not because someone gave it to you. Not because conditions are perfect. But because you've chosen to step forward anyway.

And maybe that's all any of us can do. Keep stepping. Keep questioning. Keep becoming.

The rest? We'll figure it out as we go.

This is what unapologetic living looks like...

It's not about shouting.

It's not about proving anyone wrong.

It's about showing up fully as yourself and never shrinking again.

When you stop apologizing for your standards...

When you stop diluting your voice to fit someone else's box...

When you stop measuring your worth in metrics...

You unlock a different level of freedom.

The freedom to say no without guilt.

The freedom to say yes without hesitation.

The freedom to walk into a room and not flinch, even if nobody claps.

So let this sink in:

You don't need permission to live at full volume.

You don't need applause to validate your effort.

You don't need "likes" to prove your impact.

You just need courage. The courage to bet on yourself over and over again.

The world doesn't need another copy.

It needs your original.

So step forward. Speak louder. Play bigger.

And this time? Don't apologize for any of it.

This is YOUR moment.

OWN IT

UNAPOLOGETICALLY

ACKNOWLEDGEMENTS

This book could not exist without the people who have poured into me, challenged me, and believed in me long before I believed in myself.

To my wife, Nia, and my daughter, Nylah: you are my everything. Nia, thank you for holding me down through the long nights, the doubts, and the grind that no one else sees. Your love and belief fuel me in ways I can never fully capture in words. And Nylah, you are my inspiration. Every page of this book carries a piece of the future I want you to grow up in. One where confidence, clarity, and purpose are lived unapologetically.

To my parents, Joseph and Pamela Ulmer, thank you for planting the seeds of faith, discipline, and resilience that made this journey possible. You taught me the value of hard work and the strength of character long before I understood how much it would matter. Everything I build now is rooted in the foundation you gave me.

To every coach, trainer, and athletic trainer who invested in me throughout my playing days, your lessons stretched far beyond the court and the field. You shaped my toughness, my accountability, and my understanding of what it means to lead and to serve.

To every athlete I've had the privilege to work with: you have shaped me as much as I've hoped to shape you. Your grace, your grind, and your growth have taught me more than any textbook or degree ever could. Every session, every conversation, and every story shared has helped me sharpen this message.

To the contributing authors, Demond Washington, Kyree Brown, Aaron Mercadel III, Jason Burnell, and Deontre Brown, thank you for trusting me with your stories. Your honesty and courage are reminders that vulnerability is strength, and your words will live far beyond these pages.

And finally, to anyone I will meet and impact in the future, this book is for you too. The Unapologetic Athlete movement is bigger than me. It is about all of us who continue to carry the torch, break barriers, and write legacies that last.

ABOUT THE AUTHOR

Aren J. Ulmer, PsyD. is a Certified Mental Performance Consultant (CMPC), Performance Psychology Specialist, former NCAA basketball player, and Doctor of Psychology with a specialization in Sport & Performance Psychology. He is the founder of InnerGame Performance and the creator of Unapologetic Athlete, a movement dedicated to helping athletes build confidence, clarity, and purpose that lasts far beyond the game.

Aren's journey began on the hardwood, where he lived the grind, the injuries, the doubts, and the silence that comes when the ball stops bouncing. Those experiences became the foundation for his mission: to equip athletes with the tools to embrace who they are, thrive through transition, and lead with authenticity in every arena of life.

He has delivered talks on national stages, where his powerful sessions on athlete identity, transition, and mental wellness have inspired athletes across the country. Aren's work blends lived experience with cutting-edge performance psychology, creating a playbook that challenges athletes to compete unapologetically, both on and off the court.

Beyond the work, Aren is passionate about storytelling, building platforms that amplify athlete voices, and spending time with his family. *Unapologetic Athlete* is his debut book and the cornerstone of a larger movement: empowering athletes to write their own legacy; brick by brick, chapter by chapter.

THE MOVEMENT CONTINUES

This book is only the beginning. The real work happens when you take these lessons and live them out, day after day, choice after choice, rep after rep.

Unapologetic Athlete is a movement built for athletes who refuse to be defined by stats, scores, or seasons. It is a community of people who are ready to write their story with confidence, clarity, and purpose.

If this book spoke to you, stay connected. Join the conversation. Share your story. Step into a space where athletes push boundaries, speak truth, and build legacy together.

Follow along for the ride! This is just the beginning!

**YOUR STORY IS STILL BEING WRITTEN.
LIVE IT UNAPOLOGETICALLY.**

www.ingramcontent.com/pod-product-compliance
Lightning Source LLC
Chambersburg PA
CBHW071321150726
47997CB00002B/550